OBSERVATIONS ON THE Florid Song;

OR,

SENTIMENTS ON THE *Ancient* and *Modern* Singers.

Written in *Italian*
By Pier. Francesco Tosi,
Of the *Phil-Harmonic* Academy
at *Bologna*.

Tranſlated into *Engliſh*
By Mr. GALLIARD.

Uſeful for all Performers, *Inſtrumental* as well as *Vocal*.

To which are added,
Explanatory Annotations,
and Examples in Musick.

Ornari Res ipſa negat, contenta doceri.

The Second Edition.

LONDON:
Printed for J. Wilcox, at *Virgil*'s Head, in the *Strand*. 1743.

Pier Francesco Tosi:

Observations on the Florid Song.

First published, London, 1742.

Second edition, London, 1743.
Republished Travis & Emery 2010.

Pier Francesco Tosi (1653-1732) was a singer and composer as well as an author of books on music. Born and lived in Italy for his early career, he sang and taught in London 1693-1701 and returned again in 1724. He was a founder member of the Academy of Ancient Music in 1726, an institution revived by Christopher Hogwood in 1973.

More information available in:
  Grove's Dictionary of Music and Musicians.

© 2010 Travis & Emery

Published by
Travis & Emery Music Bookshop
17 Cecil Court, London, WC2N 4EZ, England.
Tel. (+44) 20 7240 2129.
neworders@travis-and-emery.com

ISBN Hardback: 978-1-904331-51-3
Paperback: 978-1-904331-52-0

Note, By the *Ancient*, our Author means those who liv'd about thirty or forty Years ago; and by the *Modern* the late and present Singers.

N. B. *The Original was Printed at* Bologna, *in the Year* 1723.

TO ALL
Lovers of MUSICK.

LADIES and GENTLEMEN,

Ersons of Eminence, Rank, Quality, and a distinguishing Taste in any particular Art or Science, are always in View of Authors who want a Patron for that Art or Science, which they endeavour to recommend and promote. No wonder therefore, I should have

a 2 fix'd

fix'd my Mind on You, to patronize the following Treatise.

If there are Charms in Musick in general, all the reasonable World agrees, that the *Vocal* has the Pre-eminence, both from *Nature* and *Art* above the Instrumental: From *Nature*, because without doubt it was the first; from *Art*, because thereby the Voice may be brought to express Sounds with greater Nicety and Exactness than Instruments.

The Charms of the human Voice, even in Speaking, are very powerful. It is well known, that in *Oratory* a just *Modulation* of it is of the highest Consequence. The Care Antiquity took to bring it to Perfection, is a sufficient Demonstration of the Opinion they had of its Power; and every body, who has a discerning Faculty, may have experienced that sometimes a Discourse, by the Power of the *Orator*'s Voice, has made an Impression, which was lost in the Reading.

But, above all, the soft and pleasing Voice of the *fair Sex* has irresistible Charms, and adds considerably to their Beauty.

If the Voice then has such singular Prerogatives, one must naturally wish its Perfection in musical Performances, and be inclined to forward any thing that may be conducive to that end. This is the reason why I have been the more easily previ *To all Lovers*, &c.

prevail'd upon to engage in this Work, in order to make a famous *Italian Master*, who treats so well on this Subject, familiar to *England*; and why I presume to offer it to your Protection.

The Part, I bear in it, is not enough to claim any Merit; but my endeavouring to offer to your Perusal what may be entertaining, and of Service, intitles me humbly to recommend myself to your Favour: Who am,

LADIES *and* GENTLEMEN,

Your most devoted,

And most obedient

Humble Servant,

J. E. GALLIARD.

A

Prefatory Discourse,

GIVING

Some Account of the AUTHOR.

PIER. *Francesco Tosi*, the Author of the following Treatise, was an *Italian*, and a Singer of great Esteem and Reputation. He spent the most part of his Life in travelling, and by that Means heard the most eminent Singers in *Europe*,

rope, from whence, by the Help of his nice Taste, he made the following Observations. Among his many Excursions, his Curiosity was raised to visit *England*, where he resided for some time in the Reigns of King *James* the Second, King *William*, King *George* the First, and the Beginning of his present Majesty's: He dy'd soon after, having lived to above Fourscore. He had a great deal of Wit and Vivacity, which he retained to his latter Days. His manner of Singing was full of Expression and Passion; chiefly in the Stile of Chamber-Musick. The best Performers in his Time thought themselves happy when they could have an Opportunity to hear him. After he had lost his Voice, he apply'd himself more particularly to Composition; of which he has given Proof in his *Cantata's*, which are of an exquisite Taste, especially in the *Recitatives*, where he excels in the *Pathetick* and *Expression* beyond any other. He was a zealous Well-wisher to all who distinguished themselves in Musick; but rigorous to those who abused and degraded the Profession. He was very much esteemed by Persons of Rank; among whom the late Earl of *Peterborough* was one, having often met him in his Travels beyond Sea; and he was well received by his Lordship when in *England*, to Whom he dedicated this Treatise. This alone would be a sufficient Indication of his Merit, his being taken Notice of by a Person of that Quality, and distinguishing Taste. The Emperor *Joseph* gave him an honourable Employment in some part of *Italy*, and the late *Arch-Dutchess* a Church-Retirement in *Flanders*, where he died. As for his *Observations* and *Sentiments* on Singing, they must speak for themselves; and the Translation of them, it is hoped, will be acceptable to Lovers of Musick, because this particular Branch has never been treated of in so distinct and ample a Manner by any other Author. Besides, it has been thought by Persons of Judgment, that it would be of Service to make the Sentiments of our Author more universally known, when a false Taste in Musick is so prevailing; and, that these Censures, as they are passed by an *Italian* upon his own Countrymen, cannot but be looked upon as impartial. It is incontestable, that the Neglect of true Study, the sacrificing

ficing the Beauty of the Voice to a Number of ill-regulated Volubilities, the neglecting the Pronunciation and Expression of the Words, besides many other Things taken Notice of in this Treatise, are all *bad*. The Studious will find, that our Author's Remarks will be of Advantage, not only to Vocal Performers, but likewise to the Instrumental, where Taste and a Manner are required; and shew, that a little less *Fiddling* with the *Voice*, and a little more *Singing* with the *Instrument*, would be of great Service to Both. Whosoever reads this Treatise with Application, cannot fail of Improvement by it. It is hoped, that the Translation will be indulged, if, notwithstanding all possible Care, it should be defective in the Purity of the *English* Language; it being almost impossible, (considering the Stile of our Author, which is a little more figurative than the present Taste of the *English* allows in their Writings,) not to retain something of the Idiom of the Original; but where the Sense of the Matter is made plain, the Stile may not be thought so material, in Writings of this Kind.

THE AUTHOR's Dedication TO HIS Excellency the Earl of PETERBOROUGH, General of the Marines of *Great-Britain*.

My Lord,

 I Should be afraid of leaving the World under the Imputation of Ingratitude, should I any longer defer publishing the very many Favours, which *Your Lordship* so generously has bestow'd on me in *Italy*, in *Germany*, in *Flanders*, in *England*; and principally at your delightful Seat at *Parson's-Green*, where *Your Lordship* having been pleased to do me the Honour of imparting to me your Thoughts with Freedom, I have often had the Opportunity of admiring your extensive Knowledge, which almost made me overlook the Beauty and Elegance of the Place. The famous *Tulip-Tree*, in your Garden there, is not so surprising a Rarity, as the uncommon Penetration of your Judg-

Judgment, which has sometimes (I may say) foretold Events, which have afterwards come to pass. But what Return can I make for so great Obligations, when the mentioning of them is doing myself an Honour, and the very Acknowledgment has the Appearance of *Vanity?* It is better therefore to treasure them up in my Heart, and remain respectfully silent; only making an humble Request to *Your Lordship*, that you will condescend favourably to accept this mean Offering of my Observations; which I am induc'd to make, from the common Duty which lies upon every Professor to preserve Musick in its Perfection; and upon Me in particular, for having been the first, or among the first, of those who discovered the noble Genius of your potent and generous Nation for it. However, I should not have presum'd to dedicate them to a Hero adorn'd with such glorious Actions, if *Singing* was not a Delight of the Soul, or if any one had a Soul more sensible of its Charms. On which account, I think, I have a just Pretence to declare myself, with profound Obsequiousness,

YOUR LORDSHIP'S
Most humble,
Most devoted, and
Most oblig'd Servant,

Pier. Francesco Tosi.

(xviii)

THE CONTENTS.

THE Introduction. Pag. 1

CHAP. I.
Observations for one who teaches a *Soprano*. p. 10

CHAP. II.
Of the *Appoggiatura*. p. 31

CHAP. III.
Of the *Shake*. p. 41

CHAP. IV.
On *Divisions*. p. 51

CHAP.

CONTENTS.

CHAP. V.
Of *Recitative*. p. 66

CHAP. VI.
Observations for a *Student*. p. 79

CHAP. VII.
Of *Airs*. - - p. 91

CHAP. VIII.
Of *Cadences*. - p. 126

CHAP. IX.
Observations for a *Singer*. p. 140

CHAP. X.
Of *Passages* or *Graces* p. 174

BOOKS Printed for J. WILCOX, opposite the new Church in the *Strand*.

I. A Plain and compendious Method of teaching the thorough Bass after the most rational Manner, with proper Rules and Examples for Practice, by J. F. Lampe.

II. The Songs and Duetto's in the Burlesque Opera, called, The Dragon of Wantley, in Score, by J. F. Lampe, 5 s.

III. The same, adapted to the German Flute, Hautboy, or Violin, by J. F. Lampe, 3 s.

IV. The Burlesque Opera, called Margery, being a Sequel to the Dragon of Wantley, in Score, by J. F. Lampe, 6 s.

V. The Overtures and Chorus's to both these Burlesque Operas, which are to be sold alone to those Gentlemen who have the Opera's already, by J. F. Lampe, 5 s.

VI. A musical Dictionary: Being a Collection of Terms and Characters, as well Ancient as Modern. Including the historical, theoretical, and practical Parts of Musick.

We whose Names are hereunto subscribed, do approve the following Sheets, containing a Musical Dictionary, *and recommend them as very useful, and worthy the Perusal of all Lovers of Musick.*

J. C. PEPUSCH.
M. GREENE.
J. E. GALLIARD.

THE
INTRODUCTION.

THE Opinions of the ancient Historians, on the Origin of Musick, are various. *Pliny* believes, that *Amphion* was the Inventor of it; the *Grecians* maintain, that it was *Dionysius*; *Polybius* ascribes it to the *Arcadians*; *Suidas* and *Boetius* give the Glory entirely to *Pythagoras*; asserting, that from the Sound of three Hammers of different Weights at a Smith's Forge, he found out the Diatonick; after which *Timotheus*, the *Milesian*, added the

Chromatick, and *Olympicus*, or *Olympus*, the Enharmonick Scale. However, we read in holy Writ, that *Jubal*, of the Race of *Cain, fuit Pater Canentium Citharâ & Organo*, the Father of all such as handle the Harp and Organ; Instruments, in all Probability, consisting of several harmonious Sounds; from whence one may infer, Musick to have had its Birth very soon after the World.

§ 2. To secure her from erring, she called to her Assistance many Precepts of the Mathematicks; and from the Demonstrations of her Beauties, by Means of Lines, Numbers, and Proportions, she was adopted her Child, and became a Science.

§ 3. It may reasonably be supposed, that, during the Course of several thousand Years, Musick has always been the Delight of Mankind; since the excessive Pleasure, the *Lacedemonians* received from it, induced that Republick to exile the abovementioned *Milesian*, that the *Spartans*, freed from their Effeminacy, might return again to their old Oeconomy.

§ 4. But, I believe, she never appeared with so much Majesty as in the last Centuries, in the great Genius of *Palestina*, whom she left as an immortal Example to Posterity. And, in Truth, Musick, with the Sweetness of *his* Harmony, arrived at so high a Pitch, (begging Pardon of the eminent Masters of our Days) that if she was ranked only in the Number of Liberal Arts, she might with Justice contest the Pre-eminence.

§ 4. When Arts and Sciences were retrieving from the Barbarism in which they were buried, Musick chiefly took its Rise in *Flanders*, and the Composers of Musick of that Nation were dispersed all over *Europe*, to the Improvement of others. In *Italy* there arose from that School, among several others, P. *Aël. Palestina*, a Genius so extraordinary, that he is looked upon as the *Raphael* among the Musicians. He lived in Pope *Leo* the Tenth's Time; and no Musick, that we know of, is performed at the Pope's Chapel, to this Day, but of his Composition, except the famous *Miserere* of *Allegri*, who liv'd a little time after *Palestina*.

§ 5. A strong Argument offers itself to me, from that wonderful Impression, that in so distinguished a Manner is made upon our Souls by Musick, beyond all other Arts; which leads us to believe, that it is part of that Blessedness which is enjoyed in Paradise.

§ 6. Having premised these Advantages, the Merit of the Singer should likewise be distinguished, by reason of the particular Difficulties that attend him: Let a Singer have a Fund of Knowledge sufficient to perform readily any of the most difficult Compositions; let him have, besides, an excellent Voice, and know how to use it artfully; he will not, for all that, deserve a Character of Distinction, if he is wanting in a prompt Variation; a Difficulty which other Arts are not liable to.

§ 7. Finally, I say, that Poets, Painters, Sculptors, and even Composers of Musick, before they expose their Works to the Publick, have all the Time requisite to mend and polish them; but the Singer that commits an Error has no Remedy; for the Fault is committed, and past Correction.

§ 8. We may then guess at, but cannot describe, how great the Application must be of one who is obliged not to err, in unpremeditated Productions; and to manage a Voice, always in Motion, conformable to the Rules of an Art that is so difficult. I confess ingenuously, that every time I reflect on the Insufficiency of many Masters, and the infinite Abuses they introduce, which render the Application and Study of their Scholars ineffectual, I cannot but wonder, that among so many Professors of the first Rank, who have written so amply on

§ 7. Our Author seems to be a little too partial in Favour of the Singer, all momentary Productions being the same; though it must be allowed, that by reason of the Expression of the Words, any Error in Singing will be more capital, than if the same were committed on an Instrument.

Musick in almost all its Branches, there has never been one, at least that I have heard of, who has undertaken to explain in the Art of Singing, any thing more than the first Elements, known to all, concealing the most necessary Rules for Singing well. It is no Excuse to say, that the Composers intent on Composition, the Performers on Instruments intent on their Performance, should not meddle with what concerns the Singer; for I know some very capable to undeceive those who may think so. The incomparable *Zarlino*, in the third part of his Harmonick Institution, chap. 46. just began to inveigh against those, who in his time sung with some Defects, but he stopp'd; and I am apt to believe, had he gone farther, his Documents, though grown musty in two Centuries, might be of Service to the refined Taste of this our present time. But a more just Reproof is due to the Negligence of many celebrated Singers, who, having a superior Knowledge, can the less justify their Silence, even under the Title of Modesty, which ceases to be a Virtue, when it deprives the Publick of an Advantage. Moved therefore, not by a vain Ambition, but by the Hopes of being of Service to several Professors, I have determined, not without Reluctance, to be the first to expose to the Eye of the World these my few Observations; my only End being (if I succeed) to give farther Insight to the Master, the Scholar, and the Singer.

§ 9. I will, in the first Place, endeavour to shew the Duty of a Master, how to instruct a Beginner well; secondly, what is required of the Scholar; and, lastly, with more mature Reflections, to point out the way to a moderate Singer, by which he may arrive at greater Perfection. Perhaps, my Enterprize may be term'd rash, but if the Effects should not answer my Intentions, I shall at least incite some other to treat of it in a more ample and correct Manner.

§ 10. If any should say, I might be dispensed with for not publishing

Things already known to every Professor, he might perhaps deceive himself; for among these Observations there are many, which as I have never heard them made by any body else, I shall look upon as my own; and such probably they are, from their not being generally known. Let them therefore take their Chance, for the Approbation of those that have Judgment and Taste.

§ 11. It would be needless to say, that verbal Instructions can be of no Use to Singers, any farther than to prevent 'em from falling into Errors, and that it is Practice only can set them right. However, from the Success of these, I shall be encouraged to go on to make new Discoveries for the Advantage of the Profession, or (asham'd, but not surpriz'd) I will bear it patiently, if Masters with their Names to their Criticism should kindly publish my Ignorance, that I may be undeceiv'd, and thank them.

§ 12. But though it is my Design to demonstrate a great Number of Abuses and Defects of the Moderns to be met with in the Republick of Musick, in order that they may be corrected (if they can;) I would not have those, who for want of Genius, or through Negligence in their Study, could not, or would not improve themselves, imagine, that out of Malice I have painted all their Imperfections to the Life; for I solemnly protest, that though from my too great Zeal I attack their Errors without Ceremony, I have a Respect for their Persons; having learned from a *Spanish* Proverb, that Calumny recoils back on the Author. But Christianity says something more. I speak in general; but if sometimes I am more particular, let it be known, that I copy from no other Original than myself, where there has been, and still is, Matter enough to criticize, without looking for it elsewhere.

CHAP.

CHAP. I.

OBSERVATIONS *for one who teaches a* Soprano.*

HE Faults in Singing infinuate themselves so easily into the Minds of young Beginners, and there are such Difficulties in correcting them, when grown into an Habit, that it were to be wish'd, the ablest Singers would undertake the Task of Teaching, they best knowing how to conduct the Scholar from the first Elements to Perfection. But there being none, (if I mistake not) but who abhor the Thoughts of it, we must reserve them for those Delicacies of the Art, which enchant the Soul.

§ 2. Therefore the first Rudiments necessarily fall to a Master of a lower Rank, till the Scholar can sing his part at Sight; whom one would at least wish to be an honest Man, diligent and experienced, without the Defects of singing through the Nose, or in the Throat, and that

---

* The Author directs this for the Instruction of a *Soprano*, or a treble Voice, because Youth possesses that Voice mostly, and that is the Age when they should begin to study Musick. It may not be amiss to mention, that the *Soprano* is most apt to perform the Things required by our Author, and that every different Scale of Voice has something peculiarly relative to its Kind as its own Property; for a *Soprano* has generally most Volubility, and becomes it best; and also equally the Pathetick. The *Contr'Alto* more of the Pathetick than the Volubility; the *Tenor* less of the Pathetick, but more of the Volubility than the *Contr'Alto*, though not so much as the *Soprano*. The *Bass*, in general more pompous than any, but should not be so boisterous as now too often practised.

he have a Command of Voice, some Glimpse of a good Taste, able to make himself understood with Ease, a perfect Intonation, and a Patience to endure the severe Fatigue of a most tiresome Employment.

§ 3. Let a Master thus qualified, before he begins his Instructions, read the four Verses of *Virgil*, Sic vos non vobis, &c. * for they seem to be made on Purpose for him, and after having considered them well, let him consult

§ 3. By this Section, and mostly throughout the Work, one sees, the Author calculated this Treatise chiefly for the Advantage of Professors of Musick; but, notwithstanding, it appears in several Places, that his Intention is, that all Lovers of Musick should also be the better for it.

* *The Explanation of* Sic vos non vobis, *&c. for the Satisfaction of those who do not perfectly remember it.*

Virgil having composed a Distich, containing the Praise of *Augustus*, and a Compliment on his good Fortune, fixed it on the Palace Gate, without any Name subscrib'd. *Augustus* making strict Enquiry after the Author, and *Virgil*'s Modesty not suffering him to own the Verses, one *Bathyllus*, a Poet of a mean Reputation, owned himself the Author, and received Honour and Reward from the Emperor. *Virgil*, somewhat scandalized at this Accident, fixed an Hemistich in these Words (*Sic vos non vobis*) four times repeated under the other, where he had placed the former Verses. The Emperor was as diligent to have these Hemistichs filled up, but no-body appearing to do it, at length *Virgil* supplied them thus:

Hos ego Versiculos feci, tulit alter Honores;
Sic vos non vobis nidificatis aves.
Sic vos non vobis vellera fertis oves.
Sic vos non vobis mellificatis apes.
Sic vos non vobis fertis aratra boves.

i. e. These Verses I made, but another has taken the Applause of them.

So ye Birds build not your Nests
For yourselves.
So ye Sheep bear not your Wool
For yourselves.
So ye Bees make not your Honey
For yourselves.
So ye Oxen submit to the Plow
Not for yourselves.

Upon this Discovery, *Bathillus* became the Ridicule of *Rome*, and *Virgil* acquired a double Reputation.

consult his Resolution; because (to speak plainly) it is mortifying to help another to Affluence, and be in want of it himself. If the Singer should make his Fortune, it is but just the Master, to whom it has been owing, should be also a Sharer in it.

§ 4. But above all, let him hear with a disinterested Ear, whether the Person desirous to learn hath a Voice, and a Disposition; that he may not be obliged to give a strict Account to God, of the Parent's Money ill spent, and the Injury done to the Child, by the irreparable Loss of Time, which might have been more profitably employed in some other Profession. I do not speak at random. The ancient Masters made a Distinction between the Rich, that learn'd Musick as an Accomplishment, and the Poor, who studied it for a Livelihood. The first they instructed out of Interest, and the latter out of Charity, if they discovered a singular Talent. Very few modern Masters refuse Scholars; and, provided they are paid, little do they care if their Greediness ruins the Profession.

§ 5. Gentlemen Masters! *Italy* hears no more such exquisite Voices as in Times past, particularly among the Women, and to the Shame of the Guilty I'll tell the Reason: The Ignorance of the Parents does not let them perceive the Badness of the Voice of their Children, as their Necessity makes them believe, that to sing and grow rich is one and the same Thing, and to learn Musick, it is enough to have a pretty Face: " *Can you make* " *any thing of her?*"

The Distich, which *Bathillus* claim'd for his, was this:

Nocte pluit totâ, redeunt spectacula manè,
Divisum Imperium cum Jove Cæsar habet.

i. e. It rain'd all Night; in the Morning the publick Shews return: *Jove* and *Cæsar* divide the Rule of the World.

The Compliment is, that *Cæsar* designing to exhibit Sports to the People, though the preceding Night was rainy and unpromising, yet such Weather returned with the Morning, as did not disappoint the Solemnity.

§ 6. You may, perhaps, teach them with their Voice ——— Modesty will not permit me to explain myself farther.

§ 7. The Master must want Humanity, if he advises a Scholar to do any thing to the Prejudice of the Soul.

§ 8. From the first Lesson to the last, let the Master remember, that he is answerable for any Omission in his Instructions, and for the Errors he did not correct.

§ 9. Let him be moderately severe, making himself fear'd, but not hated. I know, it is not easy to find the Mean between Severity and Mildness, but I know also, that both Extremes are bad: Too great Severity creates Stubbornness, and too great Mildness Contempt.

§ 10. I shall not speak of the Knowledge of the Notes, of their Value, of Time, of Pauses, of the Accidents, nor of other such trivial Beginnings, because they are generally known.

§ 11. Besides the *C* Cliff, let the Scholar be instructed in all the other Cliffs, and in all their Situations, that he may not be liable to what often happens to some Singers, who, in Compositions *Alla Capella* *, know not how to distinguish the *Mi* from the *Fa*, without the Help of the Organ, for want of the Knowledge of the *G* Cliff; from whence such Discordancies arise in divine Service, that it is a Shame for those who grow old in their Ignorance. I must be so sincere to declare, that whoever does not give such essential Instructions, transgresses out of Omission, or out of Ignorance.

§ 12. Next let him learn to read those in *B Molle*, especially in those Com-

---

Sect. 11. Seven Cliffs necessary to be known. Pl. 1. Numb. 1. By the Help of these Cliffs any Line or Space may be what Note you please. Pl. I. Numb. 2.

* *Alla Capella*, Church-Musick, where the Flats and Sharps are not mark'd.

§ 12. It is necessary to understand the *Sol-Fa*-ing, and its Rules, which shew where the two

[18]

Compositions that have four Flats at the Cliff, and which on the sixth of the Bass require for the most part an accidental Flat, that the Scholar may find in them the *Mi*, which is not so easy to one who has studied but little, and thinks that all the Notes with a Flat are called *Fa*: for if that were true, it would be superfluous that the Notes should be six, when five of them have the same Denomination. The *French* use seven, and, by that additional Name, save their Scholars the Trouble of learning the Mutations ascending or descending; but we *Italians* have but *Ut*, *Re*, *Mi*, *Fa*, *Sol*, *La*; Notes which equally suffice throughout all the Keys, to one who knows how to read them *.

---

two Semitones lie in each Octave, Pl. I. Numb. 3. Where Flats or Sharps are marked at the Cliff, the Rule is, if one Flat, That is *Fa*; if more Flats, the last. If one Sharp, That is *Mi*; if more Sharps, the last.

* His Meaning is, that the *French* are not in the right.

§ 13.

[19]

§ 13. Let the Master do his utmost, to make the Scholar hit and sound the Notes perfectly in Tune in *Sol-Fa*-ing. One, who has not a good Ear, should not undertake either to instruct, or to sing; it being intolerable to hear a Voice perpetually rise and fall discordantly. Let the Instructor reflect on it; for one that sings out of Tune loses all his other Perfections. I can truly say, that, except in some few Professors, the modern Intonation is very bad.

§ 14. In the *Sol Fa*-ing, let him endeavour to gain by Degrees the high Notes, that by the Help of this Exercise he may acquire as much Compass of the Voice as possible. Let him take care, however, that the higher the Notes, the more it is necessary to touch them with Softness, to avoid Screaming.

§ 15. He ought to make him hit the Semitones according to the true Rules. Every one knows not that there
is

is a Semitone Major and Minor *, becauſe the Difference cannot be known by an Organ or Harpſichord, if the Keys of the Inſtrument are not ſplit. A Tone, that gradually paſſes to another, is divided into nine almoſt imperceptible Intervals, which are called Comma's, five of which conſtitute the Semitone Major, and four the Minor. Some are of Opinion, that there are no more than ſeven, and that the greateſt Number of the one half conſtitutes the firſt, and the leſs the ſecond; but this does not ſatisfy my weak Underſtanding, for the Ear would find no Difficulty to diſtinguiſh the ſeventh part of a Tone; whereas it meets with a very great one to diſtinguiſh the ninth. If one were continually to ſing only to thoſe abovemention'd Inſtruments, this Knowledge might be unneceſſary; but ſince the time that Compoſers introduced the Cuſtom of crowding the Opera's

* See § 2. and the following, in Chap. III. where the Difficulty of the *Semitone Major* and *Minor* are cleared.

with a vaſt Number of Songs accompanied with Bow-Inſtruments, it becomes ſo neceſſary, that if a *Soprano* was to ſing *D* ſharp, like *E* flat, a nice Ear will find he is out of Tune, becauſe this laſt riſes. Whoever is not ſatisfied in this, let him read thoſe Authors who treat of it, and let him conſult the beſt Performers on the Violin. In the middle parts, however, it is not ſo eaſy to diſtinguiſh the Difference; tho' I am of Opinion, that every thing that is diviſible, is to be diſtinguiſhed. Of theſe two Semitones, I'll ſpeak more amply in the Chapter of the *Appoggiatura*, that the one may not be confounded with the other.

§ 16. Let him teach the Scholar to hit the Intonation of any Interval in the Scale perfectly and readily, and keep him ſtrictly to this important Leſſon, if he is deſirous he ſhould ſing with Readineſs in a ſhort time.

§ 17. If the Maſter does not underſtand Compoſition, let him provide himſelf with good Examples of
Sol-

Sol-Fa-ing in divers Stiles, which insensibly lead from the most easy to the more difficult, according as he finds the Scholar improves; with this Caution, that however difficult, they may be always natural and agreeable, to induce the Scholar to study with Pleasure.

§ 18. Let the Master attend with great Care to the Voice of the Scholar, which, whether it be *di Petto*, or *di Testa*, should always come forth neat and clear, without passing thro' the Nose, or being choaked in the Throat; which are two the most horrible Defects in a Singer, and past all Remedy if once grown into a Habit.

§ 19. The little Experience of some that teach to *Sol-fa*, obliges the Scholar to hold out the *Semibreves* with Force on the highest Notes; the Consequence of which is, that the Glands of the Throat become daily more and more inflamed, and if the Scholar loses not his Health, he loses the treble Voice.

§ 20. Many Masters put their Scholars to sing the *Contr' Alto*, not knowing how to help them to the *Falsetto*, or to avoid the Trouble of finding it.

§ 21. A diligent Master, knowing that a *Soprano*, without the *Falsetto*, is constrained to sing within the narrow Compass of a few Notes, ought not only to endeavour to help him to it, but also to leave no Means untried, so to unite the feigned and the natural Voice, that they may not be distinguished; for if they do not perfectly unite, the Voice will be of divers * Registers, and must consequently lose its Beauty. The Extent of the

---

§ 18. *Voce di Petto* is a full Voice, which comes from the Breast by Strength, and is the most sonorous and expressive. *Voce di Testa* comes more from the Throat, than from the Breast, and is capable of more Volubility. *Falsetto* is a feigned Voice, which is entirely formed in the Throat, has more Volubility than any, but of no Substance.

§ 21. * *Register*; a Term taken from the different Stops of an Organ.

full natural Voice terminates generally upon the fourth Space, which is *C*; or on the fifth Line, which is *D*; and there the feigned Voice becomes of Use, as well in going up to the high Notes, as returning to the natural Voice; the Difficulty consists in uniting them. Let the Master therefore consider, of what Moment the Correction of this Defect is, which ruins the Scholar if he overlooks it. Among the Women, one hears sometimes a *Soprano* entirely *di Petto*, but among the Male Sex it would be a great Rarity, should they preserve it after having past the Age of Puberty. Whoever would be curious to discover the feigned Voice of one who has the Art to disguise it, let him take Notice, that the Artist sounds the Vowel *i*, or *e*, with more Strength and less Fatigue than the Vowel *a*, on the high Notes.

§ 22. The *Voce di Testa* has a great Volubility, more of the high than the lower Notes, and has a quick Shake, but subject to be lost for want of Strength.

§ 23. Let the Scholar be obliged to pronounce the Vowels distinctly, that they may be heard for such as they are. Some Singers think to pronounce the first, and you hear the second; if the Fault is not the Master's, it is of those Singers, who are scarce got out of their first Lessons; they study to sing with Affectation, as if ashamed to open their Mouths; others, on the contrary, stretching theirs too much, confound these two Vowels with the fourth, making it impossible to comprehend whether they have said *Balla* or *Bella*, *Sesso* or *Sasso*, *Mare* or *More*.

§ 24. He should always make the Scholar sing standing, that the Voice may have all its Organization free.

§ 25. Let him take care, whilst he sings, that he get a graceful Posture, and make an agreeable Appearance.

§ 26. Let him rigorously correct all Grimaces and Tricks of the Head, of the Body, and particularly of the Mouth;

Mouth; which ought to be composed in a Manner (if the Sense of the Words permit it) rather inclined to a Smile, than too much Gravity.

§ 27. Let him always use the Scholar to the Pitch of *Lombardy*, and not that of *Rome*; not only to make him acquire and preserve the high Notes, but also that he may not find it troublesome when he meets with Instruments that are tun'd high; the Pain of reaching them not only affecting the Hearer, but the Singer. Let the Master be mindful of this; for as Age advances, so the Voice declines; and, in Progress of Time, he will either sing a *Contr' Alto*, or pretending still, out of a foolish Vanity, to the Name of a *Soprano*, he will be obliged to make Application to every Composer, that the Notes may not exceed the fourth Space (*viz.* C) nor the Voice hold out on them. If all those, who teach the first Rudiments, knew how to make use of this Rule, and to unite the feigned to the natural Voice, there would not be now so great a Scarcity of *Soprano*'s.

§ 28. Let him learn to hold out the Notes without a Shrillness like a Trumpet, or trembling; and if at the Beginning he made him hold out every Note the length of two Bars, the Improvement would be the greater; otherwise, from the natural Inclination that the Beginners have to keep the Voice in Motion, and the Trouble in holding it out, he will get a Habit, and not be able to fix it, and will become subject to a Flutt'ring in the Manner of all those that sing in a very bad Taste.

§ 29. In the same Lessons, let him teach the Art to put forth the Voice, which consists in letting it swell by Degrees from the softest *Piano* to the loudest *Forte*, and from thence with the same Art return from the *Forte* to the *Piano*. A beautiful *Messa di Voce,*

§ 27. The Pitch of *Lombardy*, or *Venice*, is something more than half a Tone higher than as *Rome*.

Voce,* from a Singer that uses it sparingly, and only on the open Vowels, can never fail of having an exquisite Effect. Very few of the present Singers find it to their Taste, either from the Instability of their Voice, or in order to avoid all Manner of Resemblance of the *odious Ancients*. It is, however, a manifest Injury they do to the Nightingale, who was the Origin of it, and the only thing which the Voice can well imitate. But perhaps they have found some other of the feathered Kind worthy their Imitation, that sings quite after the New Mode.

§ 30. Let the Master never be tired in making the Scholar *Sol-fa*, as long as he finds it necessary; for if he should let him sing upon the Vowels too soon, he knows not how to instruct.

§ 31. Next, let him study on the three open Vowels, particularly on the first, but not always upon the same, as is practised now-a-days; in order, that from this frequent Exercise he may not confound one with the other, and that from hence he may the easier come to the use of the Words.

§ 32. The Scholar having now made some remarkable Progress, the Instructor may acquaint him with the first Embellishments of the Art, which are the *Appoggiatura*'s * (to be spoke of next) and apply them to the Vowels.

§ 33. Let him learn the Manner to glide with the Vowels, and to drag the Voice gently from the high to the lower Notes, which, tho' Qualifications necessary for singing well, cannot possibly be learn'd from *Sol-fa*-ing on-

---

§ 29. * A *Messa di Voce* is the holding out and swelling a Note. Vide Pl. I. Numb. 4. This being a Term of Art, it is necessary to use it, as well as *Piano* for soft, and *Forte* for loud. N. B. Our Author recommends here to use any Grace sparingly, which he does in several other Places, and with Reason; for the finest Grace too often repeated grows tiresome.

§ 32. See for *Appoggiatura* in the next Chapter.

ly, and are overlooked by the Unskilful.

§ 34. But if he should let him sing the Words, and apply the *Appoggiatura* to the Vowels before he is perfect in *Sol-fa*-ing, he ruins the Scholar.

CHAP. II.*

Of the Appoggiatura †.

MONG all the Embellishments in the Art of Singing, there is none so easy for the Master to teach, or less difficult for the

---

* This Chapter contains some Enquiries into Matters of Curiosity, and demands a little Attention. The Reader therefore is desired to postpone it to the last.

† *Appoggiatura* is a Word to which the *English* Language has not an Equivalent; it is a Note added by the Singer, for the arriving more gracefully to the following Note, either in rising or falling, as is shewn by the Examples in Notes of Musick, Pl. II. Numb. 2. The *French* express it by two different Terms, *Port de Voix* and *Appuyer*;

the Scholar to learn, than the *Appoggiatura*. This, besides its Beauty, has obtained the sole Privilege of being heard often without tiring, provided it does not go beyond the Limits prescrib'd by Professors of good Taste.

§ 2. From the Time that the *Appoggiatura* has been invented to adorn the Art of Singing, the true Reason, why it cannot be used in all Places, remains yet a Secret. After having searched for it among Singers of the first Rank in vain, I considered that Musick, as a Science, ought to have its Rules, and that all Manner of Ways should be tried to discover them. I do not flatter myself that I am arrived at it; but the Judicious will see, at least, that I am come near it. However, treating of a Matter wholly produced from my Observations, I should hope for more Indulgence in this Chapter than in any other.

§ 3. From Practice, I perceive, that from *C* to *C* by *B Quadro*, a Voice can ascend and descend gradually with the *Appoggiatura*, passing without any the least Obstacle thro' all the

---

as the *English* do by a *Prepare* and a *Lead*. The Word *Appoggiatura* is derived from *Appoggiare*, to lean on. In this Sense, you lean on the first to arrive at the Note intended, rising or falling; and you dwell longer on the Preparation, than the Note for which the Preparation is made, and according to the Value of the Note. The same in a Preparation to a Shake, or a Beat from the Note below. No *Appoggiatura* can be made at the Beginning of a Piece; there must be a Note preceding, from whence it leads.

§ 2. Here begins the Examination of the *Semitones Major* and *Minor*, which he promised in § 15. Ch. I. It may be of Satisfaction to the Studious, to set this Matter at once in a true Light; by which our Author's Doubts will be cleared, and his Reasoning the easier understood. A *Semitone Major* changes Name, Line, and Space: A *Semitone Minor* changes neither. Pl. II.

II. Numb. 1. To a *Semitone Major* one can go with a Rise or a Fall distinctly; to a *Semitone Minor* one cannot. N. B. From a *Tone Minor* the *Appoggiatura* is better and easier than from a *Tone Major*.

§ 3. These are all *Tones Major* and *Minor*, and *Semitones Major*. Pl. II. Numb. 2.

five

five *Tones*, and the two *Semitones*, that make an *Octave*.

§ 4. That from every accidental *Diezis*, or Sharp, that may be found in the Scale, one can gradually rise a *Semitone* to the nearest Note with an *Appoggiatura*, and return in the same Manner.

§ 5. That from every Note that has a *B Quadro*, or Natural, one can ascend by *Semitones* to every one that has a *B Molle*, or Flat, with an *Appoggiatura*.

§ 6. But, contrarywise, my Ear tells me, that from *F*, *G*, *A*, *C*, and *D*, one cannot rise gradually with an *Appoggiatura* by *Semitones*, when any of

---

§ 4. Because they are *Semitones Major*. Pl. II. Numb. 3.

§ 5. Because they are *Semitones Major*. Pl. II. Numb. 4.

§ 6. Because they are all *Semitones Minor*, which may be known by the abovementioned Rule, of their not changing Name, Line, nor Space. Pl. II. Numb. 5. and which makes it manifest, that a *Semitone Minor* cannot bear an *Appoggiatura*.

these five *Tones* have a Sharp annex'd to them.

§ 7. That one cannot pass with an *Appoggiatura* gradually from a third *Minor* to the Bass, to a third *Major*, nor from the third *Major* to the third *Minor*.

§ 8. That two consequent *Appoggiatura*'s cannot pass gradually by *Semitones* from one *Tone* to another.

§ 9. That one cannot rise by *Semitone*, with an *Appoggiatura*, from any Note with a Flat.

§ 10. And, finally, where the *Appoggiatura* cannot ascend, it cannot descend.

§ 11. Practice giving us no Insight into the Reason of all these Rules, let us see if it can be found out by those who ought to account for it.

---

§ 7. For the same Reason, these being *Semitones Minor*. Pl. II. Numb. 6.

§ 8. Because one is a *Semitone Major*, and the other a *Semitone Minor*. Pl. III. Numb. 7.

§ 9. Because they are *Semitones Minor*. Pl. III. Numb. 8.

§ 12. Theory teaches us, that the above-mentioned *Octave* consisting of twelve unequal *Semitones*, it is necessary to distinguish the *Major* from the *Minor*, and it sends the Student to consult the *Tetrachords*. The most conspicuous Authors, that treat of them, are not all of the same Opinion: For we find some who maintain, that from *C* to *D*, as well as from *F* to *G*, the *Semitones* are equal; and mean while we are left in Suspense.

§ 13. The Ear, however, which is the supreme Umpire in this Art, does in the *Appoggiatura* so nicely discern the Quality of the *Semitones*, that it sufficiently distinguishes the *Semitone Major*. Therefore going so agreably from *Mi* to *Fa*, (that is) from *B Quadro* to *C*, or from *E* to *F*, one ought to conclude That to be a *Semitone Major*, as it undeniably is. But whence does it proceed, that from this very *Fa*, (that is, from *F* or *C*) I cannot rise to the next Sharp, which is also a *Semitone*? It is *Minor*, says the Ear. Therefore I take it for granted, that the Reason why the *Appoggiatura* has not a full Liberty, is, that it cannot pass gradually to a *Semitone Minor*; submitting myself, however, to better Judgment.

§ 14. The *Appoggiatura* may likewise pass from one distant Note to another, provided the Skip or Interval be not deceitful; for, in that Case,

---

§ 12. The *Tone*, or *Mood*, you are in, will determine which is a *Tone Major* or *Minor*; for if you change the *Mood* or *Tone*, that which was the *Tone Major* may become the *Tone Minor*, and so *Vice versâ*: Therefore these two Examples from *C* to *D*, and from *F* to *G*, do not hold true.

§ 13. His Perplexity comes from a wrong Notion, in not distinguishing those two *Semitones*.

§ 14. All Intervals, rising with an *Appoggiatura*, arise to the Note with a sort of *Beat*, more or less; and the same, descending, arrive to the Note with a sort of *Shake*, more or less. Pl. III. Numb. 9, 10. One cannot agreeably ascend or descend the Interval of a third *Major* or *Minor*. Pl. III. Numb. 11. But gradually very well. Pl. III. Numb. 12. Examples of false or deceitful Intervals. Pl. III. Numb. 13.

whoever does not hit it sure, will shew they know not how to sing.

§ 15. Since, as I said, it is not possible for a Singer to rise gradually with an *Appoggiatura* to a *Semitone Minor*, Nature will teach him to rise a Tone, that from thence he may descend with an *Appoggiatura* to that *Semitone*; or if he has a Mind to come to it without the *Appoggiatura*, to raise the Voice with a *Messa di Voce*, the Voice always rising till he reaches it.

§ 16. If the Scholar be well instructed in this, the *Appoggiatura*'s will become so familiar to him by continual Practice, that by the Time he is come out of his first Lessons, he will laugh at those Composers that mark them, with a Design either to be thought Modern, or to shew that they understand the Art of Singing better than the Singers. If they have this Superiority over them, why do they not write down even the Graces, which are more difficult, and more essential than the *Appoggiatura*'s? But if they mark them, that they may acquire the glorious Name of a *Virtuoso alla Moda*, or a Composer in the new Stile, they ought at least to know, that the Addition of one Note costs little Trouble, and less Study. Poor *Italy!* pray tell me; do not the Singers now-a-days know where the *Appoggiatura*'s are to be made, unless they are pointed at with a Finger? In my Time their own Knowledge shewed it them. Eternal Shame to him who first introduced these foreign Puerilities into our Nation, renowned for teaching others the greater part of the polite Arts; particularly, that of Singing! Oh, how great a Weakness in those that follow the Example!

---

§ 15. So in all Cases where the Interval is deceitful. Pl. III. Numb. 14. With a *Messa di Voce*. Pl. III. Numb. 15. See for *Messa di Voce*, Chap. I. § 29, and its Note.

§ 16. In all the modern *Italian* Compositions the *Appoggiatura*'s are mark'd, supposing the Singers to be ignorant where to place them. The *French* use them for their Lessons on the *Harpsichord*, &c. but seldom for the Voice.

ple! Oh, injurious Insult to you Modern Singers, who submit to Instructions fit for Children! Let us imitate the Foreigners in those Things only, wherein they excel.

CHAP. III.

Of the Shake.

WE meet with two most powerful Obstacles in forming the *Shake*. The first embarrasses the Master; for, to this Hour there is no infallible Rule found to teach it: And the second affects the Scholar, because Nature imparts the *Shake* but to few. The Impatience of the Master joins with the Despair of the Learner, so that they decline farther Trouble about it. But in this the Master is blameable, in not doing his Duty, by leaving the Scholar in Ignorance. One must strive against Difficulties with Patience to overcome them.

[42]

§ 2. Whether the *Shake* be necessary in Singing, ask the Professors of the first Rank, who know better than any others how often they have been indebted to it; for, upon any Absence of Mind, they would have betrayed to the Publick the Sterility of their Art, without the prompt Assistance of the *Shake*.

§ 3. Whoever has a fine *Shake*, tho' wanting in every other Grace, always enjoys the Advantage of conducting himself without giving Distaste to the End or Cadence, where for the most part it is very essential; and who wants it, or has it imperfectly, will never be a great Singer, let his Knowledge be ever so great.

§ 4. The *Shake* then, being of such Consequence, let the Master, by the Means of verbal Instructions, and Examples vocal and instrumental, strive that the Scholar may attain one that is equal, distinctly mark'd, easy, and moderately quick, which are its most beautiful Qualifications.

2

[43]

§ 5. In case the Master should not know how many Sorts of *Shakes* there are, I shall acquaint him, that the Ingenuity of the Professors hath found so many Ways, distinguishing them with different Names, that one may say there are eight Species of them.

§ 6. The first is the *Shake Major*, from the violent Motion of two neighbouring Sounds at the Distance of a *Tone*, one of which may be called Principal, because it keeps with greater Force the Place of the Note which requires it; the other, notwithstanding it possesses in its Motion the superior Sound, appears no other than an Auxiliary. From this *Shake* all the others are derived.

§ 7. The second is the *Shake Minor*,

§ 5. See for the several Examples of the *Shakes*, Pl. IV.
§ 6. The first *Shake* of a *Tone*, Pl. IV. Numb. 1.
§ 7. The second *Shake* of a *Semitone Major*, Pl. IV. Numb. 2.

§ 5.

nor, consisting of a Sound, and its neighbouring *Semitone Major*; and where the one or the other of these two *Shakes* are proper, the Compositions will easily shew. From the inferior or lower Cadences, the first, or full *Tone Shake* is for ever excluded *. If the Difference of these two *Shakes* is not easily discovered in the Singer, whenever it is with a *Semitone*, one may attribute the Cause to the want of Force of the Auxiliary to make itself heard distinctly; besides, this *Shake* being more difficult to be beat than the other, every body does not know how to make it, as it should be, and Negligence becomes a Habit. If this *Shake* is not distinguished in Instruments, the Fault is in the Ear.

* See for the Meaning of superior and inferior *Cadences*, Chap. VIII. § 1. Pl. V. Numb. 3. *N. B.* From the inferior or lower Cadences, the first, or full *Tone Shake*, is not always excluded; for in a sharp Key it is always a *Tone*, and in a flat Key a *Semitone*. Pl. IV. Numb. 3.

§ 8. The third is the *Mezzo-trillo*, or the short *Shake*, which is likewise known from its Name. One, who is Master of the first and second, with the Art of beating it a little closer, will easily learn it; ending it as soon as heard, and adding a little Brilliant. For this Reason, this *Shake* pleases more in brisk and lively Airs than in the *Pathetick*.

§ 9. The fourth is the rising *Shake*, which is done by making the Voice ascend imperceptibly, shaking from Comma to Comma without discovering the Rise.

§ 10. The fifth is the descending *Shake*, which is done by making the Voice decline insensibly from Comma to Comma, shaking in such Manner, that the Descent be not distinguished. These two *Shakes*, ever

§ 8. The third the short *Shake*, Pl. IV. Numb. 4.
§ 9. The fourth the rising *Shake*, Pl. IV. Numb. 5
§ 10. The fifth the descending *Shake*, Pl. IV. Numb. 6.

since true Taste has prevailed, are no more in Vogue, and ought rather to be forgot than learn'd. A nice Ear equally abhorrs the ancient dry Stuff, and the modern Abuses.

§ 11. The sixth is the slow *Shake*, whose Quality is also denoted by its Name. He, who does not study this, in my Opinion ought not therefore to lose the Name of a good Singer; for it being only an affected Waving, that at last unites with the first and second *Shake*, it cannot, I think, please more than once.

§ 12. The seventh is the redoubled *Shake*, which is learned by mixing a few Notes between the *Major* or *Minor Shake*, which Interposition suffices to make several *Shakes* of one. This is beautiful, when those few Notes, so intermixed, are sung with Force. If then it be gently formed on the high Notes of an excellent Voice, perfect in this rare Quality, and not made use of too often, it cannot displease even Envy itself.

§ 13. The eighth is the *Trillo-Mordente*, or the *Shake* with a *Beat*, which is a pleasing Grace in Singing, and is taught rather by Nature than by Art. This is produced with more Velocity than the others, and is no sooner born but dies. That Singer has a great Advantage, who from time to time mixes it in Passages or Divisions, (of which I shall take Notice in the proper Chapter.) He, who understands his Profession, rarely fails of using it after the *Appoggiatura*; and he, who despises it, is guilty of more than Ignorance.

§ 14. Of all these *Shakes*, the two first are most necessary, and require most the Application of the Master. I know too well that it is customary to sing without *Shakes*; but the Example, of those who study but superficially, ought not to be imitated.

---

§ 11. The sixth the slow *Shake*, Pl. IV. Numb. 7.

§ 12. The seventh the redoubled *Shake*, Pl. IV. Numb. 8.

§ 13. The eighth the *Trillo-Mordente*, or *Shake* with a *Beat*, Pl. IV. Numb. 9.

§ 15. The *Shake*, to be beautiful, requires to be prepared, though, on some Occasions, Time or Taste will not permit it. But on final Cadences, it is always necessary, now on the Tone, now on the *Semitone* above its Note, according to the Nature of the Composition.

§ 16. The Defects of the *Shake* are many. The long holding-out *Shake* triumph'd formerly, and very improperly, as now the Divisions do; but when the Art grew refined, it was left to the Trumpets, or to those Singers that waited for the Eruption of an *E Viva!* or *Bravo!* from the Populace. That *Shake* which is too often heard, be it ever so fine, cannot please. That which is beat with an uneven Motion disgusts; that like the Quivering of a Goat makes one laugh; and that in the Throat is the worst: That which is produced by a Tone and its third, is disagreeable; the Slow is tiresome; and that which is out of Tune is hideous.

§ 17. The Necessity of the *Shake* obliges the Master to keep the Scholar applied to it upon all the Vowels, and on all the Notes he possesses; not only on Minims or long Notes, but likewise on Crotchets, where in Process of Time he may learn the *Close Shake*, the *Beat*, and the Forming them with Quickness in the Midst of the Volubility of Graces and Divisions.

§ 18. After the free Use of the *Shake*, let the Master observe if the Scholar has the same Facility in disusing it; for he would not be the first that could not leave it off at Pleasure.

§ 19. But the teaching where the *Shake* is convenient, besides those on

§ 19. *Shakes* are generally proper from preceding Notes descending, but not ascending, except on particular Occasions. Never too many, or too near one another; but very bad to begin with them, which is too frequently done. The using so often *Beats*, *Shakes*, and *Prepares*, is owing to Lessons on the Lute, Harpsichord, and other Instruments, whose Sounds discontinue, and therefore have Need of this Help.

Cadences, and where they are improper and forbid, is a Lesson reserv'd for those who have Practice, Taste, and Knowledge.

CHAP.

CHAP. IV.

On Divisions.

HO' *Divisions* have not Power sufficient to touch the Soul, but the most they can do is to raise our Admiration of the Singer for the happy Flexibility of his Voice; it is, however, of very great Moment, that the Master instruct the Scholar in them, that he may be Master of them with an easy Velocity and true Intonation; for when they are well executed in their proper Place, they deserve Applause, and make a Singer more universal; that is to say, capable to sing in any Stile.

§ 2. By accustoming the Voice of a Learner to be lazy and dragging, he is rendered incapable of any considerable Progress in his Profession. Whosoever has not Agility of Voice, in Compositions of a quick or lively Movement, becomes odiously tiresome; and at last retards the Time so much, that every thing he sings appears to be out of Tune.

§ 3. *Division*, according to the general Opinion, is of two Kinds, the Mark'd, and the Gliding; which last, from its Slowness and Dragging, ought rather to be called a Passage or Grace, than a *Division*.

§ 4. In regard to the first, the Master ought to teach the Scholar that light Motion of the Voice, in which the Notes that constitute the Division be all articulate in equal Proportion, and moderately distinct, that they be not too much join'd, nor too much mark'd.

§ 4. The *mark'd Divisions* should be something like the *Staccato* on the Violin, but not too much; against which a Caution will presently be given.

§ 5. The second is perform'd in such a Manner, that the first Note is a Guide to all that follow, closely united, gradual, and with such Evenness of Motion, that in Singing it imitates a certain Gliding, by the Masters called a *Slur*; the Effect of which is truly agreeable when used sparingly.

§ 6. The *mark'd Divisions*, being more frequently used than the others, require more Practice.

§ 7. The Use of the *Slur* is pretty much limited in Singing, and is confined within such few Notes ascending or descending, that it cannot go beyond a fourth without displeasing. It seems to me to be more grateful to the Ear descending, than in the contrary Motion

§ 8. The *Dragg* consists in a Succession of divers Notes, artfully mixed with the *Forte* and *Piano*. The Beauty of which I shall speak of in another Place.

§ 5. The *Gliding Notes* are like several Notes in one Stroke of the Bow on the Violin.

§ 9. If the Master hastens insensibly the Time when the Scholar sings the *Divisions*, he will find that there is not a more effectual way to unbind the Voice, and bring it to a Volubility; being however cautious, that this imperceptible Alteration do not grow by Degrees into a vicious Habit.

§ 10. Let him teach to hit the *Divisions* with the same Agility in ascending gradually, as in descending; for though this seems to be an Instruction fit only for a Beginner, yet we do not find every Singer able to perform it.

§ 11. After the gradual *Divisions*, let him learn to hit, with the greatest Readiness, all those that are of difficult Intervals, that, being in Tune and Time, they may with Justice deserve our Attention. The Study of this Lesson demands more Time and Application than any other, not so much for the great Difficulty in attaining it, as the important Consequences that attend it; and, in Fact, a Singer loses all Fear when the most difficult *Divisions* are become familiar to him.

§ 12. Let him not be unmindful to teach the Manner of mixing the *Piano* with the *Forte* in the *Divisions*; the *Glidings* or *Slurs* with the *Mark'd*, and to intermix the *Close Shake*; especially on the pointed Notes, provided they be not too near one another; making by this Means every Embellishment of the Art appear.

§ 13. Of all the Instructions relating to *Divisions*, the most considerable seems to be That, which teaches to unite the *Beats* and *short Shake* with them; and that the Master point out to him, how to execute them with Exactness of Time, and the Places where they have the best Effect: But this being not so proper for one who teaches only the first Rules, and still less for him that begins to learn them, it would be better to have postponed this (as perhaps I should have done) did I not know that there are Scholars of so quick Parts, that in a few Years become most excellent Singers, and that there is no Want of Masters qualified to instruct Disciples of the most promising Genius; besides, it appeared to me an Impropriety in this Chapter on *Divisions* (in which the *Beats* and *Close Shake* appear with greater Lustre than any other Grace) not to make Mention of them.

§ 14. Let the Scholar not be suffered to sing *Divisions* with Unevenness of Time or Motion; and let him be corrected if he marks them with the Tongue, or with the Chin, or any other Grimace of the Head or Body.

§ 15. Every Master knows, that on the third and fifth Vowel, the *Divisions* are the worst; but every one does not know, that in the best Schools the second and fourth were not permitted, when these two Vowels are pronounced close or united.

§ 16. There are many Defects in the *Divisions*, which it is necessary to know, in order to avoid them; for, besides that of the Nose or the Throat, and the others already mentioned, those are likewise displeasing which are neither mark'd nor gliding; for in that Case they cannot be said to sing, but howl and roar. There are some still more ridiculous, who mark them above Measure, and with Force of Voice, thinking (for Example) to make a *Division* upon *A*, it appears as if they said *Ha, Ha, Ha,* or *Gha, Gha, Gha*; and the same upon the other Vowels. The worst Fault of all is singing them out of Tune.

§ 17. The Master should know, that though a good Voice put forth with Ease grows better, yet by too swift a Motion in *Divisions* it becomes an indifferent one, and sometimes by the Negligence of the Master, to the Prejudice of the Scholar, it is changed into a very bad one.

§ 18. *Divisions* and *Shakes* in a *Siciliana* are Faults, and *Glidings* and *Draggs* are Beauties.

§ 19. The sole and entire Beauty of the *Division* consists in its being perfectly in Tune, mark'd, equal, distinct, and quick.

§ 20. *Divisions* have the like Fate with the *Shakes*; both equally delight in their Place; but if not properly introduced, the too frequent Repetition of them becomes tedious, if not odious.

§ 21. After the Scholar has made himself perfect in the *Shake* and the *Divisions*, the Master should let him read and pronounce the Words, free from those gross and ridiculous Errors of Orthography, by which many deprive one Word of its double Consonant, and add one to another, in which it is single.

§ 22. After having corrected the Pronunciation, let him take Care that the Words be uttered in such a Manner, without any Affectation, that they be distinctly understood, and no one Syllable be lost; for if they are not distinguished, the Singer deprives the Hearer of the greatest Part of that Delight which vocal Musick conveys by Means of the Words. For, if the Words are not heard so as to be understood, there will be no great Difference between a human Voice and a Hautboy. This Defect, tho' one of the greatest, is now-a-days more than common, to the greatest Disgrace of the Professors and the Profession; and yet they ought to know, that the Words only give the Preference to a Singer above an instrumental Performer, admitting them to be of equal Judgment and Knowledge. Let the modern Master learn to make use of this Advice, for never was it more necessary than at present.

§ 23. Let him exercise the Scholar to be very ready in joining the Syllables to the Notes, that he may never be at a Loss in doing it.

---

§ 21. The pronouncing *Eror* instead of *Error*; or *Dally* instead of *Daly*. The not distinguishing the double Consonants from the single, is an Error but too common at present.

§ 24. Let him forbid the Scholar to take Breath in the Middle of a Word, becaufe the dividing it in two is an Error againft Nature; which muft not be followed, if we would avoid being laugh'd at. In interrupted Movements, or in long *Divifions*, it is not fo rigoroufly required, when the one or the other cannot be fung in one Breath. Anciently fuch Cautions were not neceffary, but for the Learners of the firft Rudiments; now the Abufe, having taken its Rife in the modern Schools, gathers Strength, and is grown familiar with thofe who pretend to Eminence. The Mafter may correct this Fault, in teaching the Scholar to manage his Refpiration, that he may always be provided with more Breath than is needful; and may avoid undertaking what, for want of it, he cannot go through with.

§ 25. Let him fhew, in all forts of Compofitions, the proper Place where to take Breath, and without Fatigue; becaufe there are Singers who give Pain to the Hearer, as if they had an Afthma, taking Breath every Moment with Difficulty, as if they were breathing their laft.

§ 26. Let the Mafter create fome Emulation in a Scholar that is negligent, inciting him to ftudy the Leffon of his Companion, which fometimes goes beyond Genius; becaufe, if inftead of one Leffon he hears two, and the Competition does not difcountenance him, he may perhaps come to learn his Companion's Leffon firft, and then his own.

§ 27. Let him never fuffer the Scholar to hold the Mufick-Paper, in Singing, before his Face, both that the Sound of the Voice may not be obftructed, and to prevent him from being bafhful.

§ 28. Let him accuftom the Scholar to fing often in Prefence of Perfons of Diftinction, whether from Birth, Quality, or Eminence in the Profeffion, that by gradually lofing his Fear, he may acquire an Affurance, but not a Boldnefs. Affurance leads

leads to Fortune, and in a Singer becomes a Merit. On the contrary, the Fearful is most unhappy; labouring under the Difficulty of fetching Breath, the Voice is always trembling, and obliged to lose Time at every Note for fear of being choaked: He gives us Pain, in not being able to shew his Ability in publick; disgusts the Hearer, and ruins the Compositions in such a Manner, that they are not known to be what they are. A timorous Singer is unhappy, like a Prodigal, who is miserably poor.

§ 29. Let not the Master neglect to shew him, how great their Error is who make *Shakes* or *Divisions*, or take Breath on the *syncopated* or *binding* Notes; and how much better Effect the holding out the Voice has. The Compositions, instead of losing, acquire thereby greater Beauty.

§ 30. Let the Master instruct him in the *Forte* and *Piano*, but so as to use him more to the first than the second, it being easier to make one sing soft than loud. Experience shews that the *Piano* is not to be trusted to, since it is prejudicial though pleasing; and if any one has a Mind to lose his Voice, let him try it. On this Subject some are of Opinion, that there is an artificial *Piano*, that can make itself be heard as much as the *Forte*; but that is only Opinion, which is the Mother of all Errors. It is not Art which is the Cause that the *Piano* of a good Singer is heard, but the profound Silence and Attention of the Audience. For a Proof of this, let any indifferent Singer be silent on the Stage for a Quarter of a Minute when he should sing, the Audience, curious to know the Reason of this unexpected Pause, are hush'd in such a Manner, that if in that Instant he utter one Word with a soft Voice, it would be heard even by those at the greatest Distance.

§ 31. Let the Master remember, that whosoever does not sing to the

---

§ 29. See for the *syncopated*, *Ligatura*, or *binding* Notes, Pl. IV. Numb. 10.

utmost Rigour of Time, deserves not the Esteem of the Judicious; therefore let him take Care, there be no Alteration or Diminution in it, if he pretends to teach well, and to make an excellent Scholar.

§ 32. Though in certain Schools, Books of Church-Musick and of *Madrigals* lie buried in Dust, a good Master would wipe it off; for they are the most effectual Means to make a Scholar ready and sure. If Singing was not for the most part performed by Memory, as is customary in these Days, I doubt whether certain Professors could deserve the Name of Singers of the first Rank.

§ 33. Let him encourage the Scholar if he improves; let him mortify him, without Beating, for Indolence; let him be more rigorous for Negligences; nor let the Scholar ever end a Lesson without having profited something.

§ 34. An Hour of Application in a Day is not sufficient, even for one of the quickest Apprehension; the Master therefore should consider how much more Time is necessary for one that has not the same Quickness, and how much he is obliged to consult the Capacity of his Scholar. From a mercenary Teacher this necessary Regard is not to be hoped for; expected by other Scholars, tired with the Fatigue, and sollicited by his Necessities, he thinks the Month long; looks on his Watch, and goes away. If he be but poorly paid for his Teaching, --- a God-b'wy to him.

---

§ 32. *Madrigals* are Pieces in several Parts; the last in Practice were about threescore Years ago; then the Opera's began to be in Vogue, and good Musick and the Knowledge of it began to decline.

end

CHAP. V.

Of Recitative.

RECITATIVE is of three Kinds, and ought to be taught in three different Manners.

§ 2. The first, being used in Churches, should be sung as becomes the Sanctity of the Place, which does not admit those wanton Graces of a lighter Stile; but requires some *Messa di Voce*, many *Appoggiatura's*, and a noble Majesty throughout. But the Art of expressing it, is not to be learned, but from the affecting Manner of those who devoutly dedicate their Voices to the Service of God.

§ 3. The second is Theatrical, which being always accompanied with Action by the Singer, the Master is obliged to teach the Scholar a certain natural Imitation, which cannot be beautiful, if not expressed with that Decorum with which Princes speak, or those who know how to speak to Princes.

§ 4. The last, according to the Opinion of the most Judicious, touches the Heart more than the others, and is called *Recitativo di Camera*. This requires a more peculiar Skill, by reason of the Words, which being, for the most part, adapted to move the most violent Passions of the Soul, oblige the Master to give the Scholar such a lively Impression of them, that he may seem to be affected with them himself. The Scholar having finished his Studies, it will be but too

§ 4. *Musica di Camera*. Chamber, or private, Musick; where the Multitude is not courted for Applause, but only the true Judges; and consists chiefly in *Cantata's*, *Duetto's*, &c. In the Recitative of *Cantata's*, our Author excelled in a singular Manner for the pathetick Expression of the Words.

easily

easily discovered if he stands in Need of this Lesson. The vast Delight, which the Judicious feel, is owing to this particular Excellence, which, without the Help of the usual Ornaments, produces all this Pleasure from itself; and, let Truth prevail, where Passion speaks, all *Shakes*, all *Divisions* and *Graces* ought to be silent, leaving it to the sole Force of a beautiful Expression to persuade.

§ 5. The Church *Recitative* yields more Liberty to the Singer than the other two, particularly in the final Cadence; provided he makes the Advantage of it that a Singer should do, and not as a Player on the Violin.

§ 6. The Theatrical leaves it not in our Election to make Use of this Art, lest we offend in the Narrative, which ought to be natural, unless in a *Soliloquy* where it may be in the Stile of Chamber-Musick.

§ 7. The third abstains from great part of the Solemnity of the first, and contents itself with more of the second.

§ 8. The Defects and unsufferable Abuses which are heard in *Recitatives*, and not known to those who commit them, are innumerable. I will take Notice of several Theatrical ones, that the Master may correct them.

§ 9. There are some who sing *Recitative* on the Stage like That of the Church or Chamber; some in a perpetual Chanting, which is insufferable; some over-do it and make it a Barking; some whisper it, and some sing it confusedly; some force out the last Syllable, and some sink it; some sing it blust'ring, and some as if they were thinking of something else; some in a languishing Manner; others in a Hurry; some sing it through the Teeth, and others with Affectation; some do not pronounce the Words, and others do not express them; some sing it as if laughing, and some crying; some speak it, and some hiss it; some hallow, bellow, and sing it out of Tune; and, together with their Offences againſt Nature, are guilty of the greateſt Fault, in thinking themſelves above Correction.

§ 10. The *modern* Maſters run over with Negligence their Inſtructions in all Sorts of *Recitatives*, becauſe in theſe Days the Study of Expreſſion is looked upon as unneceſſary, or deſpiſed as *ancient*: And yet they muſt needs ſee every Day, that beſides the indiſpenſible Neceſſity of knowing how to ſing them, Theſe even teach how to act. If they will not believe it, let them obſerve, without flattering themſelves, if among their Pupils they can ſhew an Actor of equal Merit with *Cortona* in the Tender; * of Baron *Balarini* in the Imperious; or other famous Actors that at preſent appear, tho' I name them not; having determined in theſe Obſervations, not to mention any that are living, in whatſoever Degree of Perfection they be, though I eſteem them as they deſerve.

§ 11. A Maſter, that diſregards *Recitative*, probably does not underſtand the Words, and then, how can he ever inſtruct a Scholar in Expreſſion, which is the Soul of vocal Performance, and without which it is impoſſible to ſing well? Poor *Gentlemen Maſters*, who direct and inſtruct Beginners, without reflecting on the utter Deſtruction you bring on the Science, in undermining the principal Foundations of it! If you know not that the *Recitatives*, eſpecially in the vulgar or known Language, require thoſe Inſtructions relative to the Force of the Words, I would adviſe you to renounce the Name, and Office of *Maſters*, to thoſe who can maintain them; your Scholars will otherwiſe be made a Sacrifice to Ignorance, and not knowing how to diſtinguiſh the Lively from the Pathetick, or the Vehement from the Tender, it will be no wonder if you ſee them ſtupid

---

§ 10. *Cortona* liv'd above forty Years ago. *Balarini*, in Service at the Court of *Vienna*, much in Favour with the Emperor *Joſeph*, who made him a Baron.

on the Stage, and senseless in a Chamber. To speak my Mind freely, yours and their Faults are unpardonable; it is insufferable to be any longer tormented in the Theatres with *Recitatives*, sung in the Stile of a Choir of *Capuchin* Friars.

§ 12. The Reason, however, of not giving more Expression to the *Recitative*, in the Manner of those called *Antients*, does not always proceed from the Incapacity of the Master, or the Negligence of the Singer, but from the little Knowledge of the *modern* Composers, (we must except some of Merit) who set it in so unnatural a Taste, that it is not to be taught, acted or sung. In Justification of the Master and the Singer let Reason decide. To blame the Composer, the same Reason forbids me entering into a Matter too high for my low Understanding, and wisely bids me consider the little Insight I can boast of, barely sufficient for a Singer, or to write plain Counterpoint. But when I consider I have undertaken in these Observations, to procure diverse Advantages to vocal Performers, should I not speak of Composition, a Subject so necessary, I should be guilty of a double Fault. My Doubts in this Perplexity are resolved by the Reflection, that *Recitatives* have no Relation to Counterpoint. If That be so, what Professor knows not, that many theatrical *Recitatives* would be excellent if they were not confused one with another; if they could be learned by Heart; if they were not deficient in respect of adapting the Musick to the Words; if they did not frighten those who sing them, and hear them, with unnatural Skips; if they did not offend the Ear and Rules with the worst Modulations; if they did not disgust a good Taste with a perpetual Sameness; if, with their cruel Turns and Changes of Keys, they did not pierce one to the Heart; and, finally, if the Periods were not crippled by them who know neither Point nor Comma? I am astonished that such as these do not, for their Improvement, endea-

endeavour to imitate the *Recitatives* of those Authors, who represent in them a lively Image of Nature, by Sounds which of themselves express the Sense, as much as the very Words. But to what Purpose do I shew this Concern about it? Can I expect that these Reasons, with all their Evidences, will be found good, when, even in regard to Musick, Reason itself is no more in the *Mode?* Custom has great Power. She arbitrarily releases her Followers from the Observance of the true Rules, and obliges them to no other Study than that of the *Ritornello's*, and will not let them uselessly employ their precious Time in the Application to *Recitative*, which, according to her Precepts, are the work of the Pen, not of the Mind. If it be Negligence or Ignorance, I know not; but I know very well, that the Singers do not find their Account in it.

§ 13. Much more might still be said

§ 13. See Broken Cadences, Pl. V. Numb. 1.
——Final Cadences, Pl. V. Numb. 2.

on the Compositions of *Recitative* in general, by reason of that tedious chanting that offends the Ear with a thousand broken Cadences in every Opera, which Custom has established, though they are without Taste or Art. To reform them all, would be worse than the Disease; the introducing every time a final Cadence would be wrong: But if in these two Extremes a Remedy were necessary, I should think, that among an hundred broken Cadences, ten of them, briefly terminated on Points that conclude a Period, would not be ill employed. The Learned, however, do not declare themselves upon it, and from their Silence I must hold myself condemned.

§ 14. I return to the Master, only to put him in Mind, that his Duty is to teach Musick; and if the Scholar, before he gets out of his Hands, does not sing readily and at Sight, the Innocent is injured without Remedy from the Guilty.

§ 15. If after these Instructions, the Master does really find himself capable of communicating to his Scholar Things of greater Moment, and what may concern his farther Progress, he ought immediately to initiate him in the Study of Church-Airs, in which he must lay aside all the theatrical effeminate Manner, and sing in a manly Stile; for which Purpose he will provide him with different natural and easy *Motets* *, grand and genteel, mix'd with the Lively and the Pathetick, adapted to the Ability he has discovered in him, and by frequent Lessons make him become perfect in them with Readiness and Spirit. At the same time he must be careful that the Words be well pronounced, and perfectly understood; that the *Recitatives* be expressed with Strength, and supported without Affectation; that in the Airs he be not wanting in Time, and in introducing some Graces of good Taste; and, above all, that

* § 15. *Motets*, or Anthems.

the final Cadences of the *Motets* be performed with Divisions distinct, swift, and in Tune. After this he will teach him that Manner, the Taste of *Cantata*'s requires, in order, by this Exercise, to discover the Difference between one Stile and another. If, after this, the Master is satisfied with his Scholar's Improvement, yet let him not think to make him sing in Publick, before he has the Opinion of such Persons, who know more of singing than of flattering; because, they not only will chuse such Compositions proper to do him Honour and Credit, but also will correct in him those Defects and Errors, which out of Oversight or Ignorance the Master had not perceived or corrected.

§ 16. If Masters did consider, that from our first appearing in the Face of the World, depends our acquiring Fame and Courage, they would not so blindly expose their Pupils to the Danger of falling at the first Step.

§ 17. But if the Master's Knowledge extends no farther than the foregoing Rules, then ought he in conscience to desist, and to recommend the Scholar to better Instructions. However, before the Scholar arrives at this, it will not be quite unnecessary to discourse with him in the following Chapters, and if his Age permits him not to understand me, those, who have the Care of him, may.

CHAP. VI.

Observations for a Student.

EFORE entering on the extensive and difficult Study of the *Florid*, or *figured Song*, it is necessary to consult the Scholar's Genius; for if Inclination opposes, it is impossible to force it, and when That incites, the Scholar proceeds with Ease and Pleasure.

§ 2. Supposing then, that the Scholar is earnestly desirous of becoming a Master in so agreable a Profession, and being fully instructed in these tiresome Rudiments, besides many others that may have slipt my weak Memory; after a strict Care of his Morals, he should give the rest of his

his Attention to the Study of singing in Perfection, that by this Means he may be so happy as to join the most noble Qualities of the Soul to the Excellencies of his Art.

§ 3. He that studies Singing must consider, that Praise or Disgrace depends very much on his Voice, which if he has a Mind to preserve, he must abstain from all Manner of Disorders, and all violent Diversions.

§ 4. Let him be able to read perfectly, that he may not be put to Shame for so scandalous an Ignorance. Oh, how many are there, who had need to learn the Alphabet!

§ 5. In case the Master knows not how to correct the Faults in Pronunciation, let the Scholar endeavour to learn the best by some other Means; because, the not being born in *Tuscany*, will not excuse the Singer's Imperfection.

§ 6. Let him likewise very carefully endeavour to correct all other Faults that the Negligence of his Master may have passed over.

§ 7. With the Study of Musick, let him learn also at least the Grammar, to understand the Words he is to sing in Churches, and to give the proper Force to the Expression in both Languages. I believe I may be so bold to say, that divers Professors do not even understand their own Tongue, much less the *Latin*.

§ 8. Let him continually, by himself, use his Voice to a Velocity of Motion, if he thinks to have a Command over it, and that he may not go by the Name of a pathetick Singer.

§ 9. Let him not omit frequently to put forth, and to stop, the Voice,

---

§ 5. The Proverb is, * *Lingua* Toscana *in bocca* Romana. — This regards the different Dialects in *Italy*; as *Neapolitan*, *Venetian*, &c. the same, in Comparison, *London* to *York*, or *Somersetshire*.

§ 7. The Church-Musick in *Italy* is all in *Latin*, except *Oratorio's*, which are Entertainments in their Churches. It is therefore necessary to have some Notion of the *Latin* Tongue.

§ 10. Let him repeat his Lesson at Home, till he knows it perfectly; and with a local Memory let him retain it, to save his Master the Trouble of Teaching, and himself of studying it over again.

§ 11. Singing requires so strict an Application, that one must study with the Mind, when one cannot with the Voice.

§ 12. The unwearied Study of Youth is sure to overcome all Obstacles that oppose, though Defects were suck'd in with our Mother's Milk. This Opinion of mine is subject to strong Objections; however, Experience will defend it, provided he corrects himself in time. But if he delays it, the older he grows the more his Faults will encrease.

§ 13. Let him hear as much as he can the most celebrated Singers, and likewise the most excellent instrumental Performers; because, from the Attention in hearing them, one reaps more Advantage than from any Instruction whatsoever.

§ 14. Let him endeavour to copy from Both, that he may insensibly, by the Study of others, get a good Taste. This Advice, though extremely useful to a Student, is notwithstanding infinitely prejudicial to a Singer, as I shall shew in its proper Place.

§ 15. Let him often sing the most agreable Compositions of the best Authors, and accustom the Ear to that which pleases. I'd have a Student know, that by the abovementioned Imitations, and by the Idea of good Compositions, the Taste in Time becomes Art, and Art Nature.

§ 16. Let him learn to accompany himself, if he is ambitious of singing well. The Harpsichord is a great Incitement to Study, and by it we continually improve in our Knowledge. The evident Advantage arising to the

---

§ 14. The first Caution against imitating injudiciously the Instrumental with the Voice.

Singer from that lovely Instrument, makes it superfluous to say more on that Head. Moreover, it often happens to one who cannot play, that without the Help of another he cannot be heard, and is thereby to his Shame obliged to deny the Commands of those whom it would be to his Advantage to obey.

§ 17. Till a Singer pleases himself, it is certain he cannot please others. Therefore consider, if some Professors of no small Skill have not this Pleasure for want of sufficient Application, what must the Scholar do? Study,—and study again, and not be satisfied.

§ 18. I am almost of Opinion, that all Study and Endeavours to sing are infallibly vain, if not accompanied with some little Knowledge of Counterpoint. One, who knows how to compose, can account for what he does, and he, who has not the same Light, works in the Dark, not knowing how to sing without committing Errors. The most famous *Ancients* know the intrinsick Value of this Precept from the Effects. And a good Scholar ought to imitate them, without considering whether this Lesson be according to the *Mode* or not. For though, in these Days, one now and then hears admirable Performances, proceeding from a natural Taste, yet they are all done by Chance, but where that Taste is wanting, if they are not execrable, at least they will be very bad: For Fortune not being always at their Command, they cannot be sure to agree, neither with Time nor Harmony. This Knowledge although requisite, I would not however advise a Scholar to give himself up to an intense Application, it being certain, I should teach him the readiest way to lose his Voice; but I exhort him only to learn the princi-

---

§ 18. The *Italians* have a Saying, *Voce di Compositore*, to denote a bad or an indifferent Voice.

pal Rules, that he may not be quite in the Dark.

§ 19. To study much, and preserve a Voice in its full Beauty, are two Things almost incompatible; there is between them such a sort of Amity, as cannot last without being prejudicial to the one or the other. However, if one reflects, that Perfection in a Voice is a Gift of Nature, and in Art a painful Acquisition, it will indeed be allowed, that this latter excels in Merit, and more deserves our Praise.

§ 20. Whoever studies, let him look for what is most excellent, and let him look for it wherever it is, without troubling himself whether it be in the Stile of fifteen or twenty Years ago, or in that of these Days; for all Ages have their good and bad Productions. It is enough to find out the best, and profit by them.

§ 21. To my irreparable Misfortune, I am old; but were I young, I would imitate as much as possibly I could the *Cantabile* of those who are branded with the opprobrious Name of *Ancients*; and the *Allegro* of those who enjoy the delightful Appellation of *Moderns*. Though my Wish is vain as to myself, it will be of Use to a prudent Scholar, who is desirous to be expert in both Manners, which is the only way to arrive at Perfection; but if one was to chuse, I should freely, without Fear of being tax'd with Partiality, advise him to attach himself to the Taste of the first.

§ 22. Each Manner of Singing hath a different Degree of Eminence; the Nervous and Strong is distinguished from the Puerile and Weak, as is the Noble from the Vulgar.

§ 23. A Student must not hope for Applause, if he has not an utter Abhorrence of Ignorance.

---

§ 21. *Cantabile*, the Tender, Passionate, Pathetick; more Singing than *Allegro*, which is Lively, Brisk, Gay, and more in the executive Way.

§ 24. Whoever does not aspire to the first Rank, begins already to give up the second, and by little and little will rest contented with the lowest.

§ 25. If, out of a particular Indulgence to the Sex, so many female Singers have the Graces set down in Writing, one that studies to become a good Singer should not follow the Example; whosoever accustoms himself to have Things put in his Mouth, will have no Invention, and becomes a Slave to his Memory.

§ 26. If the Scholar should have any Defects, of the Nose, the Throat, or of the Ear, let him never sing but when the Master is by, or somebody that understands the Profession, in order to correct him, otherwise he will get an ill Habit, past all Remedy.

§ 27. When he studies his Lesson at Home, let him sometimes sing before a Looking-glass, not to be enamoured with his own Person, but to avoid those convulsive Motions of the Body, or of the Face (for so I call the Grimaces of an affected Singer) which, when once they have took Footing, never leave him.

§ 28. The best Time for Study is with the rising of the Sun; but those, who are obliged to study, must employ all their Time which can be spared from their other necessary Affairs.

§ 29. After a long Exercise, and the Attainment of a true Intonation, of a *Messa di Voce*, of *Shakes*, of *Divisions*, and *Recitative* well expressed, if the Scholar perceives that his Master cannot teach him all the Perfection of Execution required in the more refined Art of singing the Airs, or if he cannot always be by his Side, then will he begin to be sensible of the Need he has of that Study, in which the best Singer in the World is still a Learner, and must be his own Master. Supposing this Reflection just, I advise him for his first Insight, to read the follow-

following Chapter, in order thereby to reap greater Advantage from thoſe that can ſing the *Airs*, and teach to ſing them.

CHAP. VII.

Of Airs.

F whoever introduced the Cuſtom of repeating the firſt Part of the *Air*, (which is called *Da Capo*) did it out of a Motive to ſhew the Capacity of the Singer, in varying the Repetition, the Invention cannot be blam'd by Lovers of Muſick; though in reſpect of the Words it is ſometimes an Impropriety.

§ 1. Suppoſe the firſt Part expreſſed Anger, and the ſecond relented, and was to expreſs Pity or Compaſſion, he muſt be angry again in the *Da Capo*. This often happens, and is very ridiculous if not done to a real Purpoſe, and that the Subject and Poetry require it.

§ 2. By the *Ancients* beforementioned, *Airs* were sung in three different Manners; for the Theatre, the Stile was lively and various; for the Chamber, delicate and finish'd; and for the Church, moving and grave. This Difference, to very many *Moderns*, is quite unknown.

§ 3. A Singer is under the greatest Obligation to the Study of the *Airs*; for by them he gains or loses his Reputation. To the acquiring this valuable Art, a few verbal Lessons cannot suffice; nor would it be of any great Profit to the Scholar, to have a great Number of *Airs*, in which a Thousand of the most exquisite Passages of different Sorts were written down: For they would not serve for all Purposes, and there would always be wanting that Spirit which accompanies extempore Performances, and is preferable to all servile Imitations. All (I think) that can be said, is to recommend to him an attentive Observation of the Art, with which the best Singers regulate themselves to the Bass, whereby he will become acquainted with their Perfections, and improve by them. In order to make his Observations with the greater Exactness, let him follow the Example of a Friend of mine, who never went to an Opera without a Copy of all the Songs, and, observing the finest Graces, confin'd to the most exact Time of the Movement of the Bass, he made thereby a great Progress.

§ 4. Among the Things worthy of Consideration, the first to be taken Notice of, is the Manner in which all *Airs* divided into three Parts are to be sung. In the first they require nothing but the simplest Ornaments, of a good Taste and few, that the Composition may remain simple, plain, and pure; in the second they expect, that to this Purity some artful Gra-

---

§ 3. It is supposed, the Scholar is arrived to the Capacity of knowing Harmony and Counterpoint.

§ 4. The general dividing of *Airs* described, to which the Author often refers.

ces be added, by which the Judicious may hear, that the Ability of the Singer is greater; and, in repeating the *Air*, he that does not vary it for the better, is no great Master.

§ 5. Let a Student therefore accustom himself to repeat them always differently, for, if I mistake not, one that abounds in Invention, though a moderate Singer, deserves much more Esteem, than a better who is barren of it; for this last pleases the Connoisseurs but for once, whereas the other, if he does not surprise by the Rareness of his Productions, will at least gratify your Attention with Variety.

§ 6. The most celebrated among the *Ancients* piqued themselves in varying every Night their Songs in the Opera's, not only the *Pathetick*, but also the *Allegro*. The Student, who is not well grounded, cannot undertake this important Task.

§ 5. With due Deference to our Author, it may be feared, that the Affectation of Singing with Variety has conduced very much to the introducing a bad Taste.

§ 7. Without varying the *Airs*, the Knowledge of the Singers could never be discovered; but from the Nature and Quality of the Variations, it will be easily discerned in two of the greatest Singers which is the best.

§ 8. Returning from this Digression to the above-mentioned repeating the first Part of the *Air* with Variation, the Scholar will therein find out the Rules for Gracing, and introducing Beauties of his own Invention: These will teach him, that Time, Taste, and Skill, are sometimes of but small Advantage to one who is not ready at *extempore* Embellishments; but they should not allow, that a Superfluity of them should prejudice the Composition, and confound the Ear.

§ 9. Let a Scholar provide himself with a Variety of Graces and Embellishments, and then let him make use of them with Judgment; for if he

§ 8. Continuation of the general dividing *Airs* in § 4. The End of this Section is a seasonable Corrective of the Rule prescribed in the foregoing fifth Section.

observes,

observes, he will find that the most celebrated Singers never make a Parade of their Talent in a few Songs; well knowing, that if Singers expose to the Publick all they have in their Shops, they are near becoming Bankrupts.

§ 10. In the Study of *Airs*, as I have before said, one cannot take Pains enough; for, though certain Things of small Effect may be omitted, yet how can the Art be called perfect if the Finishing is wanting?

§ 11. In *Airs* accompanied only with a Bass, the Application of him who studies Graces is only subject to Time, and to the Bass; but in those, that are accompanied with more Instruments, the Singer must be also attentive to their Movement, in order to avoid the Errors committed by those who are ignorant of the Contrivance of such Accompaniments.

§ 12. To prevent several false Steps in singing the *Airs*, I would strongly inculcate to a Student, first, never to give over practising in private, till he is secure of committing no Error in Publick; and next, that at the first Rehearsal the *Airs* be sung without any other Ornaments than those which are very natural; but with a strict Attention, to examine at the same time in his Mind, where the artificial ones may be brought in with Propriety in the second; and so from one Rehearsal to another, always varying for the better, he will by Degrees become a great Singer.

§ 13. The most necessary Study for singing *Airs* in Perfection, and what is more difficult than any other, is to seek for what is easy and natural, as well as of beautiful Inventions. One who has the good Fortune to unite two such rare Talents, with an agreeable *putting forth* of the Voice, is a very happy Singer.

§ 14. Let him, who studies under the Disadvantage of an ungrateful Genius, remember for his Comfort, that singing in Tune, Expression, *Messa di Voce*, the *Appoggiatura's*, *Shakes*, *Divisions*, and accompanying himself, are

are the principal Qualifications; and no such insuperable Difficulties, but what may be overcome. I know, they are not sufficient to enable one to sing in Perfection; and that it would be Weakness to content one's self with only singing tolerably well; but Embellishments must be called in to their aid, which seldom refuse the Call, and sometimes come unsought. Study will do the Business.

§ 15. Let him avoid all those Abuses which have overspread and established themselves in the *Airs*, if he will preserve Musick in its Chastity.

§ 16. Not only a Scholar, but every Singer ought to forbear *Caricatura's*, or mimicking others, from the very bad Consequences that attend them. To make others laugh, hardly gains any one Esteem, but certainly gives Offence; for no-body likes to appear ridiculous or ignorant. This Mimicking arises for the most part from a concealed Ambition to shew their own Merit, at another's Expence; not without a Mixture of Envy and Spight. Examples shew us but too plainly the great Injury they are apt to do, and that it well deserves Reproof; for Mimickry has ruin'd more than one Singer.

§ 17. I cannot sufficiently recommend to a Student the exact keeping of Time; and if I repeat the same in more than one Place, there is more than one Occasion that moves me to it; because, even among the Professors of the first Rank there are few, but what are almost insensibly deceived into an Irregularity, or hastening of Time, and often of both; which though in the Beginning is hardly perceptible, yet in the Progress of the *Air* becomes more and more so, and at the last the Variation, and the Error is discovered.

§ 18. If I do not advise a Student to imitate several of the *Moderns* in their Manner of singing *Airs*, it is from their Neglect of keeping Time, which ought to be inviolable, and not sacrificed to their beloved Passages and Divisions.

§ 19. The Presumption of some Singers is not to be borne with, who expect that an whole *Orchestre* should stop in the midst of a well-regulated Movement, to wait for their ill-grounded Caprices, learned by Heart, carried from one Theatre to another, and perhaps stolen from some applauded female Singer, who had better Luck than Skill, and whose Errors were excused in regard to her Sex.——Softly, softly with your Criticism, says one; this, if you do not know it, is called Singing after the *Mode*——Singing after the *Mode?*——I say, you are mistaken. The stopping in the *Airs* at every second and fourth, and on all the sevenths and sixths of the Bass, was a bad Practice of the ancient Masters, disapproved fifty Years ago by *Rivani*, called *Ciecolino* *, who with invincible Reasons shewed the proper Places for Embellishments, without begging Pauses. This Precept was approved by several eminent Persons, among whom was Signor *Pistochi* *, the most famous of our, and all

* § 19. *Rivani*, called *Ciecolino*, must have written some Treatise on Time, which is not come to us, therefore no further Account can be given of him.

* *Pistochi* was very famous above fifty Years ago, and refined the Manner of singing in *Italy*, which was then a little crude. His Merit in this is acknowledged by all his Countrymen, contradicted by none. Briefly, what is recounted of him, is, that when he first appeared to the World, and a Youth, he had a very fine treble Voice, admired and encouraged universally, but by a dissolute Life lost it, and his Fortune. Being reduced to the utmost Misery, he entered into the Service of a Composer, as a Copyist, where he made use of the Opportunity of learning the Rules of Composition, and became a good Proficient. After some Years, he recovered a little Glimpse of Voice, which by Time and Practice turned into a fine *Contr'Alto*. Having Experience on his Side, he took Care of it, and as Encouragement came again, he took the Opportunity of travelling all *Europe* over, where hearing the different Manners and Tastes, he appropriated them to himself, and formed that agreeable Mixture, which he produced in *Italy*, where he was imitated and admired. He at last past many Years, when in an affluent Fortune, at the Court of *Anspach*, where he had a Stiall preceding Times, who has made himself immortal, by shewing the way of introducing Graces without transgressing against Time. This Example alone, which is worth a Thousand, (O my rever'd *Moderns!*) should be sufficient to undeceive you. But if this does not satisfy you, I will add, that *Sifacio* * with his mellifluous Voice embrac'd this Rule; that *Buzzolini* * of incomparable Judgment highly esteemed it: After them *Luigino* † with his soft and amorous Stile followed their Steps; likewise *Signora Boschi* ‡, who, to the Glory of her Sex, has made it appear, that Women, who study, may instruct even Men of some Note. That *Signora Lotti* ||, strictly

---

a Stipend, and lived an agreeable easy Life; and at last retired to a Convent in *Italy*. It has been remark'd, that though several of his Disciples shewed the Improvement they had from him, yet others made an ill use of it, having not a little contributed to the Introduction of the *modern* Taste.

* *Sifacio*, famous beyond any, for the most singular Beauty of his Voice. His Manner of Singing was remarkably plain, consisting particularly in the *Messa di Voce*, the putting forth his Voice, and the Expression.

There is an *Italian* Saying, that an hundred Perfections are required in an excellent Singer, and he that hath a fine Voice has ninety-nine of them.

It is also certain, that as much as is allotted to Volubility and Tricks, so much is the Beauty of the Voice sacrificed; for the one cannot be done without Prejudice to the other.

Sifacio got that Name from his acting the Part of *Syphax* the first time he appeared on the Stage. He was in *England* when famous, and belonged to King *James* the Second's Chapel. After which he returned to *Italy*, continuing to be very much admired, but at last was waylaid, and murthered for his Indiscretion.

* *Buzzolini*, the Name known, but no Particulars of him.

† *Luigino*, in the Service of the Emperor *Joseph*, and a Scholar of *Pistochi*.

‡ *Signora Boschi* was over in *England* in Queen *Anne*'s Time; she sung one Season in the Opera's, returned to *Venice*, and left her Husband behind for several Years; he sung the Bass. She was a Mistress of Musick, but her Voice was on the Decay when she came here.

|| *Santini*, afterwards *Signora Lotti*. She was famous above forty Years ago, and appeared at several Courts in *Germany*, where she was sent for;

strictly keeping to the same Rules, with a penetrating Sweetness of Voice, gained the Hearts of all her Hearers. If Persons of this Rank, and others at present celebrated all over *Europe*, whom I forbear to name; if all these have not Authority enough to convince you, that you have no Right to alter the Time by making Pauses, consider at least, that by this Error in respect of Time, you often fall into a greater, which is, that the Voice remains unaccompanied, and deprived of Harmony; and thereby becomes flat and tiresome to the best Judges. You will perhaps say in Excuse, that few Auditors have this Discernment, and that there are Numbers of the others, who blindly applaud every thing that has an Appearance of Novelty. But whose Fault is this? An Audience, that applauds what is blameable, cannot justify your Faults by their Ignorance; it is your Part to set them right, and, laying aside your ill-grounded Practice, you should own, that the Liberties you take are against Reason, and an Insult upon all those instrumental Performers that are waiting for you, who are upon a Level with you, and ought to be subservient only to the Time. In short, I would have you reflect, that the abovementioned Precept will always be of Advantage to you; for though under the neglecting of it, you have a Chance to gain Applause of the Ignorant only; by observing it, you will justly merit that of the Judicious, and the Applause will become universal.

§ 20. Besides the Errors in keeping Time, there are other Reasons, why a Student should not imitate the *modern* Gentlemen in singing *Airs*, since it

---

for; then retired to *Venice*, where she married *Signor Lotti*, Chapel-Master of St. *Mark*.

All these Singers, though they had a Talent particular to themselves, they could, however, sing in several sorts of Stile; on the contrary, one finds few, but what attempt nothing that is out of their Way. A modern Singer of the good Stile, being asked, whether such and such Compositions would not please at present in *Italy*? No doubt, said he, they would, but where are the Singers that can sing them?

it plainly appears that all their Application now is to divide and subdivide in such a Manner, that it is impossible to understand either Words, Thoughts, or Modulation, or to distinguish one *Air* from another, they singing them all so much alike, that, in hearing of one, you hear a Thousand.——— And must the *Mode* triumph? It was thought, not many Years since, that in an Opera, one rumbling *Air* full of Divisions was sufficient for the most gurgling Singer to spend his Fire *; but the Singers of the present Time are not of that Mind, but rather, as if they were not satisfied with transforming them all with a horrible Metamorphosis into so many Divisions, they, like Racers, run full Speed, with redoubled Violence to their final Cadences, to make Reparation for the Time they think they have lost during the Course of the *Air*. In the following Chapter, on the tormented and tortured Cadences, we shall shortly see the good Taste of the *Mode*; in the mean while I return to the Abuses and Defects in *Airs*.

§ 21. I cannot positively tell, who that *Modern* Composer, or that ungrateful Singer was, that had the Heart to banish the delightful, soothing, *Pathetick* from *Airs*, as if no longer worthy of their Commands, after having done them so long and pleasing Service. Whoever he was, it is certain, he has deprived the Profession of its most valuable Excellence. Ask all the Musicians in general, what their Thoughts are of the *Pathetick*, they all agree in the same Opinion, (a thing that seldom happens) and answer, that the *Pathetick* is what is most delicious to the Ear, what most sweetly affects the Soul, and is the strongest Basis of Harmony. And must we be deprived of these Charms, without knowing the Reason why? Oh! I understand you: I ought not to ask the Mas-

---

§ 20. Those tremendous *Airs* are called in *Italian*, *un Aria di Bravura*; which cannot perhaps be better translated into *English*, than a *Hectoring* Song.

Masters, but the Audience, those capricious Protectors of the *Mode*, that cannot endure this; and herein lies my Mistake. Alas! the *Mode* and the Multitude flow like Torrents, which when at their Height, having spent their Violence, quickly disappear. The Mischief is in the Spring itself; the Fault is in the Singers. They praise the *Pathetick*, yet sing the *Allegro*. He must want common Sense that does not see through them. They know the first to be the most Excellent, but they lay it aside, knowing it to be the most difficult.

§ 22. In former times divers *Airs* were heard in the Theatre in this delightful Manner, preceded and accompanied with harmonious and well-modulated Instruments, that ravished the Senses of those who comprehended the Contrivance and the Melody; and if sung by one of those five or six eminent Persons abovementioned, it was then impossible for a human Soul, not to melt into Tenderness and Tears from the violent Motion of the Affections. Oh! powerful Proof to confound the idoliz'd *Mode!* Are there in these Times any, who are moved with Tenderness, or Sorrow? ——No, (say all the Auditors) no; for, the continual singing of the *Moderns* in the *Allegro* Stile, though when in Perfection That deserves Admiration, yet touches very slightly one that hath a delicate Ear. The Taste of the *Ancients* was a Mixture of the *Lively* and the *Cantabile*, the Variety of which could not fail giving Delight; but the *Moderns* are so pre-possessed with Taste in *Mode*, that rather than comply with the former, they are contented to lose the greatest Part of its Beauty. The Study of the *Pathetick* was the Darling of the former; and Application to the most difficult Divisions is the only Drift of the latter. *Those* perform'd with more Judgment; and *These* execute with greater Boldness. But since I have presum'd to compare the most celebrated Singers in both Stiles, pardon me if I conclude with saying, that the *Moderns* are arrived

rived at the highest Degree of Perfection in singing to the *Ear*; and that the *Ancients* are inimitable in singing to the *Heart*.

§ 23. However, it ought not to be denied, but that the best Singers of these times have in some Particulars refined the preceding Taste, with some Productions worthy to be imitated; and as an evident Mark of Esteem, we must publickly own, that if they were but a little more Friends to the *Pathetick* and the *Expressive*, and a little less to the *Divisions*, they might boast of having brought the Art to the highest Degree of Perfection.

§ 24. It may also possibly be, that the extravagant Ideas in the present Compositions, have deprived the abovementioned Singers of the Opportunity of shewing their Ability in the *Cantabile*; in as much as the *Airs* at present in vogue go Whip and Spur with such violent Motions, as take away their Breath, far from giving them an Opportunity of shewing the Exquisiteness of their Taste. But, good God! since there are so many *modern* Composers, among whom are some of Genius equal, and perhaps greater than the best *Ancients*, for what Reason or Motive do they always exclude from their Compositions, the so-much-longed-for *Adagio*? Can its gentle Nature ever be guilty of a Crime? If it cannot gallop with the *Airs* that are always running Post, why not reserve it for those that require Repose, or at least for a compassionate one, which is to assist an unfortunate Hero, when he is to shed Tears, or die on the Stage? ———No, Sir, No; the grand *Mode* demands that he be quick, and ready to burst himself in his Lamentations, and weep with Liveliness. But what can one say? The Resentment of the *modern* Taste is not appeased with the Sacrifice of the *Pathetick* and the *Adagio* only, two inseparable Friends, but goes so far, as to prescribe those *Airs*, as Confederates, that have not the *Sharp* third. Can any thing be more absurd? *Gentlemen Composers*, (I do not speak to the eminent, but with all due Respect) Musick in my Time has chang'd its Stile three times: The first which pleased on the Stage, and in the Chamber, was that of *Pier. Simone* *, and of *Stradella* †; the second is of the best that are now living;

§ 24. * *Pierre Simone Agostini* lived about threescore Years ago. Several *Cantata's* of his Composition are extant, some of them very difficult, not from the Number of *Divisions* in the vocal Part, but from the Expression, and the surprising Incidents, and also the Execution of the Basses. He seems to be the first that put Basses with so much Vivacity; for *Charissimi* before him composed with more Simplicity, tho' he is reckoned to be one of the first, who enlivened his Musick in the Movements of his Basses. Of *Pierre-Simone* nothing more is known but that he loved his Bottle, and when he had run up a Bill in some favourite Place, he composed a *Cantata*, and sent it to a certain Cardinal, who never failed sending him a fixed Sum, with which he paid off his Score.

† *Alessandro Stradella* lived about *Pier. Simone*'s Time, or very little after. He was a most excellent Composer, superior in all Respects to the foregoing, and endowed with distinguishing personal Qualifications. It is reported, that his favourite Instrument was the Harp, with which he sometimes accompanied his Voice, which was agreeable. To hear such a Composer play on the Harp, must have been what we can have no Notion of, by what we now hear. He ended his Life fatally, for he was murthered. The Fact is thus related. Being at *Genoa*, a Place where the Ladies are allowed to live with more Freedom than in any other Part of *Italy*, *Stradella* had the Honour of being admitted into a noble Family, the Lady whereof was a great Lover of Musick. Her Brother, a wrong-headed Man, takes Umbrage at *Stradella*'s frequent Visits there, and forbids him going upon his Peril, which Order *Stradella* obeys. The Lady's Husband not having seen *Stradella* at his House for some Days, reproaches him with it. *Stradella*, for his Excuse, tells him his Brother-in-law's Order, which the Nobleman is angry with, and charges him to continue his Visits as formerly; he had been there scarce three or four Times, but one Evening going Home, attended by a Servant and a Lanthorn, four Ruffians rushed out, the Lady's Brother one among them, and with *Stiletts* or Daggers stabb'd him, and left him dead upon the Place. The People of *Genoa* all in a Rage sought for the Murtherer, who was forced to fly, his Quality not being able to protect him. In another Account

living *; and I leave others to judge whether they are *Modern*. But of your Stile, which is not quite established yet in *Italy*, and which has yet gained no Credit at all beyond the *Alps*, those that come after us will soon give their Opinion; for *Modes* last not long. But if the Profession is to continue, and end with the World, either you yourselves will see your Mistake, or your Successors will re-

---

of him, this Particularity is mentioned; that the Murderers pursued him to *Rome*, and on Enquiry learned, that an *Oratorio* of his Composition was to be performed that Evening; they went with an Intent to execute their Design, but were so moved with his Composition, that they rather chose to tell him his Danger, advised him to depart, and be upon his Guard. But, being pursued by others, he lost his Life. His Fate has been lamented by every Body, especially by those who knew his Merit, and none have thought him deserving so sad a Catastroph .

* When *Tosi* writ this, the Composers in Vogue were *Scarlatti*, *Bononcini*, *Gasparini*, *Mancini*, &c. The last and modern Stile has pretty well spread itself all over *Italy*, and begins to have a great Tendency to the same beyond the *Alps*, as he calls it.

form

form it. Wou'd you know how? By banishing the Abuses; and recalling the first, second, and third *Mood* *, to relieve the fifth, sixth, and eighth, which are quite jaded. They will revive the fourth and seventh now dead to you, and buried in Churches, for the final Closes. To oblige the Taste of the Singers and the Hearers, the *Allegro* will now and then be mixed with the *Pathetick*. The *Airs* will not always be drowned with the Indiscretion of the Instruments, that hide the artful Delicacy of the *Piano*, and the soft Voices, nay, even all Voices which will not bawl: They will no longer bear being teased with

---

* The *Moods*, here spoken of, our Author has not well explained. The Foundation he goes upon are the eight Church *Moods*. But his Meaning and Complaint is, that commonly the Compositions are in *C*, or in *A*, with their Transpositions, and that the others are not used or known. But to particularize here what the *Moods* are, and how to be used, is impossible, for that Branch only would require a large Treatise by itself.

Uni-

Unisons *, the Invention of Ignorance, to hide from the Vulgar the Insufficiency and Inability of many Men and Women Singers: They will recover the instrumental Harmony now lost: They will compose more for the Voice than the Instruments: The part for the Voice will no more have the Mortification to resign its Place to the Violins: The *Soprano's* and *Contr'Alto's* will no more sing the *Airs* in the Manner of the Bass, in Spight of a thousand *Octaves*: And, finally, their *Airs* will be more affecting, and less alike; more studied, and less painful to the Singer; and so much the more grand, as they are remote from the Vulgar. But, methinks, I hear it said, that the theatrical Licence is great,

* The *Airs*, sung in Unison with the Instruments, were invented in the *Venetian* Opera's, to please the *Barcaroles*, who are their Watermen; and very often their Applause supports an Opera. The *Roman* School always distinguished itself, and required Compositions of Study and Care. How it is now at *Rome* is doubtful; but we do not hear that there are any *Corelli's*.

and that the *Mode* pleases, and that I grow too bold. And may I not reply, that the Abuse is greater, that the Invention is pernicious, and that my Opinion is not singular? Am I the only Professor who knows that the best Compositions are the Cause of singing well, and the worst very prejudicial? Have we not more than once heard that the Quality of the Compositions has been capable, with a few Songs, of establishing the Reputation of a middling Singer, and destroying That of one who had acquired one by Merit? That Musick, which is composed by one of Judgment and Taste, instructs the Scholar, perfects the Skilful, and delights the Hearer. But since we have opened the Ball, let us dance.

§ 25. He that first introduced Musick on the Stage, probably thought to lead her to a Triumph, and raise her to a Throne. But who would ever have imagined, that in the short Course of a few Years, she should be reduced to the fatal Circumstance of seeing her own Tragedy? Ye pompous Fabricks of the Theatres! We should look upon you with Horror, being raised from the Ruins of Harmony: You are the Origin of the Abuses, and of the Errors: From You is derived the *modern* Stile, and the Multitude of Ballad-makers: You are the only Occasion of the Scarcity of judicious and well-grounded Professors, who justly deserve the Title of Chapel-Master *; since the poor Counterpoint † has been condemned, in this corrupted Age, to beg for a Piece of Bread in Churches, whilst the Ignorance of many exults on the Stage, the most part of the Composers have been prompted from Avarice, or Indigence, to abandon in such Manner the true Study, that one may foresee (if not succoured by those few, that still gloriously sustain its dearest Precepts) Musick, after having lost the Name of Science, and a Companion of Philosophy, will run the Risque of being reputed unworthy to enter into the sacred Temples, from the Scandal given there, by their Jiggs, Minuets, and Furlana's *; and, in fact, where the Taste is so deprav'd, what would make the Difference between the Church-Musick, and the Theatrical, if Money was received at the Church Doors?

§ 26. I know that the World honours with just Applause some, tho' few Masters, intelligent in both

---

§ 25. * *Maestro di Capella*, Master of the Chapel, the highest Title belonging to a Master of Musick. Even now the Singers in *Italy* give the Composers of Opera's the Title of *Signior Maestro* as a Mark of their Submission.

† *Contrapunto*, Counterpoint, or Note against Note, the first Rudiments of Composition.

* *Furlana*. A sort of a Country Dance, or *Cheshire*-Round.

It is reported, that the Church-Musick in *Italy*, far from keeping that Majesty it ought, is vastly abused the other way; and some Singers have had the Impudence to have other Words put to favourite Opera *Airs*, and sung them in Churches. This Abuse is not new, for St. *Augustin* complains of it; and *Palestina* prevented in his Time Musick from being banished the Churches.

Stiles,

Stiles, to whom I direct the Students, in order to their singing well; and if I confine the Masters to so small a Number, I do beg Pardon of those who should be comprehended therein; hoping easily to obtain it, because an involuntary Error does not offend, and an eminent Person knows no other Envy but virtuous Emulation. As for the Ignorant, who for the most part are not used to indulge any, but rather despise and hate every thing they do not comprehend, they will be the Persons from whom I am to expect no Quarter.

§ 27. To my Misfortune, I asked one of this sort, from whom he had learned the *Counterpoint?* he answered immediately, from the Instrument. (*i. e.* the Harpsichord)——Very well. I asked farther, in what *Tone* have you composed the Introduction of your Opera? ——— What *Tone!* what *Tone!* (breaking in upon me abruptly) with what musty Questions are you going to disturb my Brains? One may easily perceive from what School you come. The *Moderns*, if you do not know it, acknowledge no other *Tone* but one *; they laugh, with Reason, at the silly Opinion of those who imagine there are two, as well as at those who maintain, that their being divided into *Authentick* and *Plagal*, they become Eight, (and more if there were need) and prudently leave it to every body's Pleasure to compose as they like best. The World in your Time was asleep, and let it not displease you, if our merry and brisk Manner has awakened it with a Gayety so pleasing to the Heart, that it incites one to dance. I would have you likewise be lively before you die, and, abandoning your uncouth Ideas, make it appear, that old Age can be pleased with the Productions of Youth; other-

§ 27 * *Tono*, or *Mood*, and sometimes means the Key. Our Author in this Section is fond of a Pun, which cannot well be translated. *Tono* is sometimes writ *Tuono*, and *Tuono* signifies Thunder; therefore the Ignorant answers, he knows no other *Tuono* but that which is preceded by Lightning.

wise you will find, that you will be condemned by your own Words, that Ignorance hates all that is excellent. The polite Arts have advanced continually in Refinement, and if the rest were to give me the Lie, Musick would defend me Sword in Hand; for she cannot arrive at a higher Pitch. Awake therefore, and, if you are not quite out of your Senses, hearken to me; and you will acknowledge that I speak candidly to you; and for a Proof, be it known to you——

§ 28. That our delicious Stile has been invented to hide with the fine Name of *Modern* the too difficult Rules of the *Counterpoint*, cannot be denied.

§ 29. That there is an inviolable Rule amongst us, to banish for ever the *Pathetick*, is very true; because we will have no Melancholy.

§ 30. But, that we should be told by the old *Bashaws*, that we strive who can produce most extravagant Absurdities never heard before, and that we brag to be the Inventors of them ourselves, are the malign Reflections of those who see us exalted. Let Envy burst. You see, that the general Esteem which we have acquired, gives it for us; and if a Musician is not of our Tribe, he will find no Patron or Admirer. But since we are now speaking in Confidence and with Sincerity, who can sing or compose well, without our Approbation? Let them have ever so much Merit (you know it) we do not want Means to ruin him; even a few Syllables will suffice: It is only saying, He is an *Ancient*.

§ 31. Tell me, I beseech you, who, without us, could have brought Musick to the Height of Happiness, with no greater Difficulty than taking from the *Airs* that tiresome Emulation of the first and second Violin, and of the Tenor? Is there any that ever durst usurp the Glory of it? We, we are those, who by our Ingenuity have raised her to this Degree of Sublimity, in taking also from her that noisy murmuring of the fundamental Basses, in such Manner, —— (mark me well, and learn) that if in an *Orchestre* there were an hundred Violins, we are capable of composing in such a Manner, that all and every one shall play the very *Air* which the Voice sings. What say you to that? Can you have the Face to find Fault with us?

§ 32. Our most lovely Method, that obliges none of us to the painful Study of the Rules; which does not disquiet the Mind with the Anxiety of Speculation, nor delude us with the Study of reducing them into Practice; that does not prejudice the Health; that enchants the Ear *à la Mode*; that finds those who love it, who prize it, and who pay for it the Weight in Gold; and dare you to criticise upon it?

§ 33. What shall we say of the obscure and tedious Compositions of those whom you celebrate as the Top of the Universe, tho' your Opinion goes for nothing? Don't you perceive that those old-fashioned Crabbednesses are disgustful? We should be great Fools to grow pale, and become paralytick in studying and finding out in the Scores, the Harmony, the *Fugues*, their *Reverses*, the *Double Counterpoint*, the Multiplication of Subjects, to contract them closer, to make *Canons*, and such other dry Stuff, that are no more in *Mode*, and (what is worse) are of little Esteem, and less Profit. What say you now to this, *Master Critick*? Have you comprehended me?—— Yes, Sir. Well, what Answer do you make me? —— None.

§ 34. Really, I am astonished, O beloved Singers, at the profound Lethargy in which you remain, and which is so much to your Disadvantage. 'Tis You that ought to awaken, for now is the Time, and tell the Composers of this Stamp, that your Desire is to Sing, and not to Dance.

CHAP. VIII.

Of Cadences*.

THE *Cadences*, that terminate the *Airs*, are of two Sorts. The Composers call the one *Superior*, and the other *Inferior*. To make myself better understood by a Scholar, I mean, if a *Cadence* were in *C* natural, the Notes of the first would be *La, Sol, Fa*; and those of the second *Fa, Mi, Fa*. In *Airs* for a single Voice, or in *Recitatives*, a Singer may chuse which of these *Closes* or *Cadences* pleases him best; but if in Concert with other Voices, or accompanied with Instruments, he must not change the Superior for the Inferior, nor this with the other.

§ 2. It would be superfluous to speak of the broken *Cadences*, they being become familiar even to those who are not Professors of Musick, and which serve at most but in *Recitatives*.

§ 3. As for those *Cadences* that fall a fifth, they were never composed in the old Stile for a *Soprano*, in an *Air* for a single Voice, or with Instruments, unless the Imitation of some Words had obliged the Composer thereto. Yet these, having no other Merit, but of being the easiest of all, as well for the Composer as for the Singer, are at present the most prevailing.

§ 4. In the Chapter on *Airs*, I have exhorted the Student to avoid that Torrent of *Passages* and *Divisions*,

---

* *Cadences*; or, principal *Closes* in *Airs*.
§ 1. For superior and inferior *Cadences*, see Pl. V. Numb. 3.

§ 2. Broken *Cadences*, see Example, Chap. V. § 13, and its Note.
§ 3. *Cadences* that fall a Fifth, with and without Words, Pl. V. Numb. 4 and 5.

so much in the *Mode*; and did engage myself also, to give my weak Sentiments on the *Cadences* that are now current; and I am now ready: But, however, with the usual Protestation of submitting them, with all my other Opinions, to the Tribunal of the Judicious, and those of Taste, from whence there is no Appeal; that they, as sovereign Judges of the Profession, may condemn the Abuses of the *modern Cadences*, or the Errors of my Opinion.

§ 5. Every *Air* has (at least) three *Cadences*, that are all three final. Generally speaking, the Study of the Singers of the present Times consists in terminating the *Cadence* of the first Part with an overflowing of *Passages* and *Divisions* at Pleasure, and the *Orchestre* waits; in that of the second the Dose is encreased, and the *Orchestre* grows tired; but on the last *Cadence*, the Throat is set a going, like a Weather-cock in a Whirlwind, and the *Orchestre* yawns. But why must the World be thus continually deafened with so many *Divisions*? I must (with your Leave, *Gentlemen Moderns*) say in Favour of the Profession, that good Taste does not consist in a continual Velocity of the Voice, which goes thus rambling on, without a Guide, and without Foundation; but rather, in the *Cantabile*, in the putting forth the Voice agreably, in *Appoggiatura's*, in Art, and in the true Notion of Graces, going from one Note to another with singular and unexpected Surprizes, and stealing the Time exactly on the true *Motion* of the Bass. These are the principal and indispensible Qualities which are most essential to the singing well, and which no musical Ear can find in your capricious *Cadences*. I must still add, that very *anciently* the Stile of the Singers was insupportable,

§ 5. By the *Final Cadences* here mentioned, the first is at the End of the first Part of the *Air*; the Second at the End of the second Part; and the Third at the end of the first Part, when repeated again, or at the *Da Capo*, as it is always expressed in *Italian*.

(as I have been informed by the Master who taught me to *Sol fa*) by reason of the Number of *Passages* and *Divisions* in their *Cadences*, that never were at an end, as they are now; and that they were always the same, just as they are now. They became at last so odious, that, as a Nusance to the Sense of Hearing, they were banished without so much as attempting their Correction. Thus will it also happen to These, at the first Example given by a Singer whose Credit is established, and who will not be seduced by a vain popular Applause. This Reformation the succeeding Professors of Eminence prescribed to themselves as a Law, which perhaps would not have been abolished, were they in a Condition to be heard; but the Opulency of some, Loss of the Voice, Age, and Death of others, has deprived the Living from hearing what was truly worthy our Admiration in Singing. Now the Singers laugh at the Reformers, and their Reformation of the *Passages* in the *Cadences*; and, on the contrary, having recalled them from their Banishment, and brought them on the Stage, with some little *Caricatura* to boot, they impose them on the Ignorant for rare Inventions, and gain themselves immense Sums; it giving them no Concern that they have been abhorr'd and detested for fifty or sixty Years, or for an hundred Ages. But who can blame them? However, if Reason should make this Demand of them, with what unjust Pretence can you usurp the Name of *Moderns*, if you sing in a most *Ancient* Stile? Perhaps, you think that these Overflowings of your Throat are what procure you Riches and Praises? Undeceive yourselves, and thank the great Number of Theatres, the Scarcity of excellent Performers, and the Stupidity of your Auditors. What could they answer? I know not. But let us call them to a stricter Account.

§ 6. *Gentlemen Moderns*, can you possibly deny, but that you laugh among yourselves, when you have Recourse to your long-strung *Passages* in the *Cadences*, to go a begging for Applause from the blind Ignorant? You call this Trick by the Name of an *Alms*, begging for Charity as it were for those *E Viva's*, which, you very well know, you do not deserve from Justice: And in return you laugh at your Admirers, tho' they have not Hands, Feet, nor Voice enough to applaud you. Is this Justice? Is this Gratitude? ——— Oh! if they ever should find you out! My beloved Singers, tho' the Abuses of your *Cadences* are of use to you, they are much more prejudicial to the Profession, and are the greatest Faults you can commit; because at the same time you know yourselves to be in the Wrong. For your own Sakes undeceive the World, and employ the rare Talent you are endowed with on Things that are worthy of you. In the mean while I will return with more Courage to my Opinions.

§ 7. I should be very desirous to know, on what Foundation certain *Moderns* of Reputation, and great Name, do on the superior *Cadences* always make the *Shake* on the third in *Alt* to the final Note; since the *Shake* (which ought to be resolved) cannot be so in this Case, by reason of that very third, which being the sixth of the Bass hinders it, and the *Cadence* remains without a Resolution. If they should go so far as to imagine, that the best Rules depended on the *Mode*, I should notwithstanding think, they might sometimes appeal to the Ear, to know if That was satisfied with a *Shake* beaten with the seventh and the sixth on a Bass which makes the *Cadence*; and I am sure it would answer, No. From the Rules of the *Ancients* we learn, that the *Shake* is to be prepared on the sixth of the Bass, that after it the fifth may be heard, for that is its proper Place.

§ 8. Some others of the same Rank make their *Cadences* in the Manner of the Basses, which is, in falling a fifth,

§ 7. For the resolved and unresolved *Cadences*, see Pl. V. Numb. 6 and 7.

[134]

with a Passage of swift Notes descending gradually, supposing that by this Means they cover the *Octaves*, which, tho' disguised, will still appear.

§ 9. I hold it also for certain, that no Professor of the first Rank, in any *Cadence* whatsoever, can be allowed to make *Shakes*, or *Divisions*, on the last Syllables but one of these Words, ---*Confonderò*---*Amerò*, &c. for they are Ornaments that do not suit on those Syllables which are short, but do well on the Antecedent.

§ 10. Very many of the second Class end the inferior *Cadences* in the *French* Manner without a *Shake* *, either for want of Ability to make one, or from its being easy to copy them, or from their Desire of finding out something that may in Appearance support the Name of *Modern*. But in Fact they are mistaken; for the *French* do not leave out the *Shake* on the inferior *Cadences*, except in the *Pathe-*

§ 9. See for the Examples, Pl. V. Numb. 8.
§ 10. * See Example, Pl. VI. Numb 1.

tick

[135]

tick Airs; and our *Italians*, who are used to over-do the *Mode*, exclude it every where, tho' in the *Allegro* the *Shake* is absolutely necessary. I know, that a good Singer may with Reason abstain from the *Shake* in the *Cantabile*; however, it should be rarely; for if one of those *Cadences* be tolerable without that pleasing Grace, it is absolutely impossible not to be tired at length, with a Number one after another that die suddenly.

§ 11. I find, that all the *Moderns* (let them be Friends or Foes to the *Shake*) in the inferior *Cadences* beforementioned go with an *Appoggiatura* to the final Note, on the penultimate Syllable of a Word; and this likewise is a Defect, it appearing to me, that on such Occasions the *Appoggiatura* is not pleasing but on the last Syllable, after the Manner of the *Ancients*, or of those who know how to sing.

§ 11. See Example. Pl. VI. Numb. 2.
N. B. An *Appoggiatura* cannot be made on an unaccented Syllable.

§ 12.

§ 12. If, in the inferior *Cadences*, the best Singers of these Days think they are not in the wrong in making you hear the final Note before the Bass †, they deceive themselves grossly; for it is a very great Error, hurts the Ear, and is against the Rules; and becomes doubly so, going (as they do) to the same Note with an *Appoggiatura*, the which either ascending or descending, if not after the Bass *, is always very bad.

§ 13. And is it not worst of all, to torment the Hearers with a thousand *Cadences* all in the same Manner? From whence proceeds this Sterility, since every Professor knows, that the surest way of gaining Esteem in Singing is a Variety in the Repetition?

§ 14. If among all the *Cadences* in the *Airs*, the last allows a moderate Liberty to the Singer, to distinguish the end of them, the Abuse of it is sufferable. But it grows abominable, when the Singer persists with his tiresome Warbling, nauseating the Judicious, who suffer the more, because they know that the Composers leave generally in every *final Cadence* some Note, sufficient to make a discreet Embellishment; without seeking for it out of Time, without Taste, without Art, and without Judgment *.

§ 15. I am still more surprised when I reflect, that the *modern* Stile, after having exposed all the *Cadences* of the theatrical *Airs* to the Martyrdom of a perpetual Motion, will likewise have the Cruelty to condemn to the same Punishment not Those in the *Cantata's* only, but also the *Cadences* of their *Recitatives*. Do these Singers pretend, by their not distinguishing the Chamber-Musick from the immoderate *Gargling* of the Stage, to expect the vulgar *E Viva's* in the Cabinet of Princes?

---

§ 12. † See for Examples, Pl. VI. Numb. 3. and * Numb. 4.

§ 14. * Some, after a tender and passionate *Air*, make a lively merry *Cadence*; and, after a brisk *Air*, end it with one that is doleful.

§ 16. Let a sensible Student avoid this Example, and with this Example the Abuses, the Defects, and every other Thing that is mean and common, as well in the *Cadences* as elsewhere.

§ 17. If, the inventing particular *Cadences* without injuring the Time, has been one of the worthy Employments of the *Ancients* (so call'd) let a Student revive the Use of it; endeavouring to imitate them in their Skill of somewhat anticipating the Time; and remember, that Those, who understand the Art of Gracing, do not wait to admire the Beauty of it in a Silence of the Bass.

§ 18. Many and many other Errors are heard in the *Cadences* that were *Antique*, and which are now become *Modern*; they were ridiculous then, and are so now; therefore considering, that to change the Stile is not always to improve it, I may fairly conclude, that what is bad is to be corrected by Study, and not by the *Mode*.

§ 19. Now let us for a while leave at Rest the Opinions of the aforesaid *Ancients*, and the supposed *Moderns*, to take Notice what Improvement the Scholar has made, since he is desirous of being heard. Well then, let him attend, before we part with him, to Instructions of more Weight, that he may at least deserve the Name of a good Singer, though he may not arrive at that of an eminent one.

CHAP.

CHAP. IX.

Observations for a Singer *

Behold the Singer now appearing in Publick, from the Effects of his Application to the Study of the foregoing Lessons. But to what Purpose does he appear? Whoever, in the great Theatre of the World, does not distinguish himself, makes but a very insignificant Figure.

§ 2. From the cold Indifference perceived in many Singers, one would believe that the Science of Musick implored their Favour, to be received by them as their most humble Servant.

§ 3. If too many did not persuade themselves that they had studied sufficiently, there would not be such a Scarcity of the Best, nor such a Swarm of the Worst. These, because they can sing by Heart three or four *Kyrie's* *, think they are arrived at the *Non plus ultra*; but if you give them a *Cantata* to sing, that is even easy, and fairly written, they, instead of complying as they ought, will tell you with an impudent Face, that Persons of their Degree are not obliged to sing in the vulgar Tongue at Sight. And who can forbear laughing? For a Musician knowing that the Words, let them be either *Latin* or *Italian*, do not change the Form of the Notes, must immediately conclude, that this pert Answer of the great Man proceeds

---

* Though this Chapter regards Singers who make it their Profession, and particularly those who sing on the Stage, yet there are many excellent Precepts interspersed, that are of Use to Lovers of Musick.

§ 3. *Kyrie*, the first Word of the Mass-Musick in the Cathedral Stile, is not so difficult to them as the *Cantata's*; and the *Latin* in the Service, being familiar to them, saves them the Trouble of attending to the Words.

ceeds from his not being able to sing at Sight, or from his not knowing how to read; and he judges right.

§ 4. There are an infinite Number of others, who wish and sigh for the Moment that eases them from the painful Fatigue of their first Studies, hoping to have a Chance to make one in the Crowd of the second Rate; and stumbling by good Luck on something that gives them Bread, they immediately make a Legg to Musick and its Study, not caring whether the World knows they are, or are not among the Living. These do not consider that *Mediocrity* in a Singer means *Ignorance*.

§ 5. There are also several who study nothing but the Defects, and are endow'd with a marvelous Aptness to learn them all, having so happy a Memory as never to forget them. Their Genius is so inclined to the Bad, that

---

§ 4. *Thomas Morley*, (who lived above an hundred Years ago) in the third Part of his Treatise, pag. 179, speaking of *Motetts* or Anthems, complains thus: --- ' But I see not
' what Passions or Motions it can stir up, being
' as most Men doe commonlie Sing, --- leaving
' out the Ditty --- as it were a Musicke made
' onely for Instruments, which will indeed shew
' the Nature of the Musick, but never carry
' the Spirit and (as it were) that lively Soule
' which the Ditty giveth; but of this enough.
' And to return to the expressing of the Ditty,
' the Matter is now come to that State, that
' though a Song be never so wel made, and
' never so aptly applyed to the Words, yet
' shall you hardly find Singers to expresse it as
' it ought to be; for most of our Church-men,
' (so they can crie louder in the Quire then
' their Fellowes) care for no more; whereas,
' by the contrarie, they ought to study how to
' vowel and sing clean, expressing their Words
' with Devotion and Passion, whereby to draw
' the Hearer as it were in Chaines of Gold by
' the Eares to the Consideration of holy Things.
' But this, for the most part, you shall find a-
' mongst them, that let them continue never so
' long in the Church, yea though it were twen-
' tie Years, they will never study to sing better
' than they did the first Day of their Prefer-
' ment to that Place; so that it seems, that
' having obtained the Living which they sought
' for, they have little or no Care at all, either
' of their own Credit, or wel discharging of
' that Dutie whereby they have their Mainte-
' nance.'

if by Gift of Nature they had the beſt of Voices, they would be diſcontented if they could not find ſome Means to make it the worſt.

§ 6. One of a better Spirit will endeavour to keep better Company. He will be ſenſible of the Neceſſity of farther Diſcoveries, of farther Inſtructions, and even of another Maſter, of whom, beſides the Art of Singing, he would be glad to learn how to behave himſelf with good Breeding. This, added to the Merit acquired by his Singing, may give him Hopes of the Favour of Princes, and of an univerſal Eſteem.

§ 7. If he aims at the Character of a young Man of Wit and Judgment, let him not be vulgar or too bold.

§ 8. Let him ſhun low and diſreputable Company; but, above all, ſuch as abandon themſelves to ſcandalous Liberties.

§ 9. That Profeſſor ought not to be frequented, though excellent in this Art, whoſe Behaviour is vulgar and diſcreditable, and who cares not, provided he makes his Fortune, whether it be at the Expence of his Reputation.

§ 10. The beſt School is the Nobility, from whom every thing that is genteel is to be learned; but when a Muſician finds that his Company is not proper, let him retire without repining, and his Modeſty will be to his Commendation.

§ 11. If he ſhould not meet with a Gratification from the Great, let him never complain; for it is better to get but little, than to loſe a great deal, and that is not ſeldom the Caſe. The beſt he can do, is to be aſſiduous in ſerving them, that at leaſt he may hope for the Pleaſure of ſeeing them for once grateful, or be convinced for ever of their being ungrateful.

§ 12. My long and repeated Travels have given me an Opportunity of being acquainted with moſt of the Courts of *Europe*, and Examples, more than my Words, ſhould perſuade every able Singer to ſee them alſo; but without yielding up his Liberty ty to their Allurements: For Chains, though of Gold, are still Chains; and they are not all of that precious Metal: Besides, the several Inconveniencies of Disgrace, Mortifications, Uncertainty; and, above all, the Hindrance of Study.

§ 13. The golden Age of Musick would be already at an End, if the Swans did not make their Nests on some Theatres in *Italy*, or on the royal Banks of the *Thames*. O dear *London!* ——— On the other Streams, they sing no more as they used to do their sweet Notes at their expiring; but rather sadly lament the Expiration of those august and adorable Princes, by whom they were tenderly belov'd and esteemed. This is the usual Vicissitude of Things in this World; and we daily see, that whatever is sublunary must of Necessity decline.

§ 13. In *Italy*, the Courts of *Parma, Modena, Turin*, &c. and in *Germany*, the Courts of *Vienna, Bavaria, Hanover, Brandenbourg, Palatine, Saxony*, &c.

Let us leave the Tears to the Heart, and return to the Singer.

§ 14. A discreet Person will never use such affected Expressions as, *I cannot sing To-day;* ——— *I've got a deadly Cold*; and, in making his Excuse, falls a Coughing. I can truly say, that I have never in my Life heard a Singer own the Truth, and say, *I'm very well To-day*: They reserve the unseasonable Confession to the next Day, when they make no Difficulty to say, *In all my Days my Voice was never in better Order than it was Yesterday*. I own, on certain Conjunctures, the Pretext is not only suitable, but even necessary; for, to speak the Truth, the indiscreet Parsimony of some, who would hear Musick for Thanks only, goes so far, that they think a Master is immediately obliged to obey them *gratis*, and that the Refusal is an Offence that deserves Resentment and Revenge. But if it is a Law human and divine, that every Body should live by their honest Labour, what barbarous Custom obliges a Musician to serve without a Recompence? A curſed Over-bearing; O ſordid Avarice!

§ 15. A Singer, that knows the World, diſtinguiſhes between the different Manners of Commanding; he knows how to refuſe without diſobliging, and how to obey with a good Grace; not being ignorant, that one, who has his Intereſt moſt at Heart, ſometimes finds his Account in ſerving without a Gratification.

§ 16. One, who ſings with a Deſire of gaining Honour and Credit, cannot ſing ill, and in time will ſing better; and one, who thinks on nothing but Gain, is in the ready way to remain ignorant.

§ 17. Who would ever think, (if Experience did not ſhew it) that a Virtue of the higheſt Eſtimation ſhould prejudice a Singer? And yet, whilſt Preſumption and Arrogance triumph, (I'm ſhock'd to think on't) amiable Humility, the more the Singer has of it, the more it depreſſes him.

§ 18. At firſt Sight, Arrogance has the Appearance of Ability; but, upon a nearer View, I can diſcover Ignorance in Maſquerade.

§ 19. This Arrogance ſerves them ſometimes, as a politick Artifice to hide their own Failings: For Example, certain Singers would not be unconcern'd, under the Shame of not being able to ſing a few Barrs at Sight, if with Shrugs, ſcornful Glances, and malicious ſhaking of their Heads, they did not give the Auditors to underſtand, that thoſe groſs Errors are owing to him that accompanies, or to the *Orcheſtre*.

§ 20. To humble ſuch Arrogance, may it never meet with that Incenſe which it expects.

§ 21. Who could ſing better than the Arrogant, if they were not aſhamed to ſtudy?

§ 22. It is a Folly in a Singer to grow vain at the firſt Applauſes, without reflecting whether they are given by Chance, or out of Flattery; and if he thinks he deſerves them, there is an End of him.

§ 23. He should regulate his Voice according to the Place where he sings; for it would be the greatest Absurdity, not to make a Difference between a small Cabinet and a vast Theatre.

§ 24. He is still more to be blam'd, who, when singing in two, three, or four Parts, does so raise his Voice as to drown his Companions; for if it is not Ignorance, it is something worse.

§ 25. All Compositions for more than one Voice ought to be sung strictly as they are written; nor do they require any other Art but a noble Simplicity. I remember to have heard once a famous *Duetto* torn into Atoms by two renown'd Singers, in Emulation; the one proposing, and the other by Turns answering, that at last it ended in a Contest, who could produce the most Extravagancies.

§ 26. The Correction of Friends, that have Knowledge, instructs very much; but still greater Advantage may be gain'd from the ill-natur'd Criticks; for, the more intent they are to discover Defects, the greater Benefit may be receiv'd from them without any Obligation.

§ 27. It is certain, that the Errors corrected by our Enemies are better cured, than those corrected by ourselves; for we are apt to indulge our Faults, nor can we so easily perceive them.

§ 28. He that sings with Applause in one Place only, let him not have too good an Opinion of himself; let him often change Climates, and then he will judge better of his Talent.

§ 29. To please universally, Reason will tell you, that you must always sing well; but if Reason does not inform you, Interest will persuade you to conform to the Taste of that Nation (provided it be not too deprav'd) which pays you.

---

§ 23. There have been such, who valued themselves for shaking a Room, breaking the Windows, and stunning the Auditors with their Voice.

§ 25. The renowned Abbot *Steffani*, so famous for his *Duetto's*, would never suffer such luxuriant Singers to perform any of them, unless they kept themselves within Bounds.

§ 30. If he that sings well provokes Envy, by singing better he will get the Victory over it.

§ 31. I do not know if a perfect Singer can at the same time be a perfect Actor; for the Mind being at once divided by two different Operations, he will probably incline more to one than the other: It being, however, much more difficult to sing well than to act well, the Merit of the first is beyond the second. What a Felicity would it be, to possess both in a perfect Degree!

§ 32. Having said, a Singer should not copy, I repeat it now with this Reason; that to copy is the part of a Scholar, that of a Master is to invent.

---

§ 31. *Nicolini*, who came the first time into *England* about the Year 1708, had both Qualities, more than any that have come since. He acted to Perfection, and did not sing much inferior. His Variations in the *Airs* were excellent; but in his *Cadences* he had a little of the antiquated Tricks. *Valentini*, (who was here at the same Time) a Scholar of *Pistochi*, though not so powerful in Voice or Action as *Nicolini*, was more chaste in his Singing.

§ 33. Let it be remembered by the Singer, that copying comes from Laziness, and that none copy ill but out of Ignorance.

§ 34. Where Knowledge with Study makes one a good Singer, Ignorance with one single Copy makes a thousand bad ones; however, among these there are none that will acknowledge her for a Teacher.

§ 35. If many of the female Singers (for whom I have due Respect) would be pleased to consider, that by copying a good one, they are become very bad ones, they would not appear so ridiculous on the Stage for their Affectation in presuming to sing the *Airs* of the Person they copy, with the same Graces. In this great Error, (if it does not proceed from their Masters) they seem to be govern'd by Instinct, like the inferior Creatures, rather than by Reason; for That would shew them, that we may arrive at Applause by different ways, and past Examples, as well as one at this present fent, * make us fenfible, that two Women would not be equally eminent if the one copy'd the other.

§ 36. If the Complaifance, which is due to the fair Sex, does not excufe the Abufe of copying when it proves prejudicial to the Profeffion, what ought one then to fay of thofe Men, who, inftead of inventing, not only copy others of their own Sex, but alfo Women ? Foolifh and fhameful!--- Suppofing an Impoffibility, *viz.* that a Singer has arrived at copying in fuch a Manner as not to be diftinguifhed from the Original, fhould he attribute to himfelf a Merit which does not belong to him, and drefs himfelf out in the Habits of another without being afraid of being ftripp'd of them ?

§ 37. He that rightly knows how to copy in Mufick, takes nothing but the Defign; becaufe that Ornament, which we admire when *natural*, immediately lofes its Beauty when *artificial*.

§ 38. The moft admired Graces of a Profeffor ought only to be imitated, and not copied ; on Condition alfo, that it does not bear not even fo much as a Shadow of a Refemblance of the Original; otherwife, inftead of a beautiful Imitation, it will become a defpicable Copy.

§ 39. I cannot decide, which of the two deferves moft to be defpifed, one who cannot imitate a good Singer without *Caricatura's*, or He that cannot imitate any well but bad ones.

§ 40. If many Singers knew, that a bad Imitation is a contagious Evil, to which one who ftudies is not liable, the World would not be reduc'd to the Misfortune of feeing in a *Carnaval* but one Theatre provided with eminent Performers, without Hopes of

---

§ 35. * The two Women, he points at, are *Cuzzoni* and *Fauftina*.

§ 40. The *Carnaval* is a Feftival in *Italy*, particularly celebrated at *Venice* from *Chriftmafs* to *Lent*, when all Sorts of Diverfions are permitted ; and at that Time there are fometimes three different Theatres for Opera's only.

an approaching Remedy. Let them take it for their Pains. Let the World learn to applaud Merit; and (not to use a more harsh Expression) be less complaisant to Faults.

§ 41. Whoever does not know how to steal the Time in Singing, knows not how to Compose, nor to Accompany himself, and is destitute of the best Taste and greatest Knowledge.

§ 42. The stealing of Time, in the *Pathetick*, is an honourable Theft in one that sings better than others, provided he makes a Restitution with Ingenuity.

§ 41. Our Author has often mentioned Time; the Regard to it, the Strictness of it, and how much it is neglected and unobserv'd. In this Place speaking of stealing the Time, it regards particularly the Vocal, or the Performance on a single Instrument in the *Pathetick* and *Tender*; when the Bass goes an exactly regular Pace, the other Part retards or anticipates in a singular Manner, for the Sake of Expression, but after That returns to its Exactness, to be guided by the Bass. Experience and Taste must teach it. A mechanical Method of going on with the Bass will easily distinguish the Merit of the other Manner.

§ 43. An Exercise, no less necessary than this, is That of agreably *putting forth* of the Voice, without which all Application is vain. Whosoever pretends to obtain it, must hearken more to the Dictates of the Heart, than to those of Art.

§ 44. Oh! how great a Master is the Heart! Confess it, my beloved Singers, and gratefully own, that you would not have arrived at the highest Rank of the Profession if you had not been its Scholars; own, that in a few Lessons from it, you learned the most beautiful Expressions, the most refin'd Taste, the most noble Action, and the most exquisite Graces: Own, (though it be hardly credible) that the Heart corrects the Defects of Nature, since it softens a Voice that's harsh, betters an indifferent one, and perfects a good one: Own, when the Heart sings you cannot dissemble, nor has Truth a greater Power of persuading: And, lastly, do you convince the World, (what is not in my Power to do) that from the Heart alone you have learn'd, that *Je ne fçai quoy*, that pleasing Charm, that so subtily passes from Vein to Vein, and makes its way to the very Soul.

§ 45. Though the way to the Heart is long and rugged, and known but to few, a studious Application will, notwithstanding, master all Obstacles.

§ 46. The best Singer in the World continues to study, and persists in it as much to maintain his Reputation, as he did to acquire it.

§ 47. To arrive at that glorious End, every body knows that there is no other Means than Study; but That does not suffice; it is also necessary to know in what Manner, and with whose Assistance, we must pursue our Studies.

§ 48. There are now-a-days as many Masters as there are Professors of Musick in any Kind; every one of them teaches, I don't mean the first Rudiments only, (That would be an Affront to them;) I am now speaking of those who take upon them the part of a Legislator in the most finished part in Singing; and should we then wonder that the good Taste is near lost, and that the Profession is going to Ruin? So mischievous a Pretension prevails not only among those, who can barely be said to sing, but among the meanest instrumental Performers; who, though they never sung, nor know how to sing, pretend not only to teach, but to perfect, and find some that are weak enough to be imposed on. But, what is more, the instrumental Performers of some Ability imagine that the beautiful Graces and Flourishes, with their nimble Fingers, will have the same Effect when executed with the Voice; but it will not do *. I should be the first to con-

§ 48. A farther Animadversion against imitating Instruments with the Voice.

* Many Graces may be very good and proper for a Violin, that would be very improper for a Hautboy; and so with every Species of Instruments that have something peculiar. It is a very great Error (too much in Practice) for the Voice, (which should serve as a Standard to be imitated by Instruments,) to copy all the Tricks practised on the several Instruments, to its greatest Detriment.

demn the magisterial Liberty I take, were it meant to give Offence to such Singers and instrumental Performers of Worth, who know how to sing, perform, and instruct; but my Correction aims no farther than to the Petulancy of those that have no Capacity, with these few Words, *Age quod agis*; which (for those who do not understand *Latin*) is as much as to say, —— Do You mind your *Sol-fa*; and You, your Instrument.

§ 49. If sometimes it does happen, that an indifferent Master should make an excellent Disciple, it is then incontestable, that the Gift of Nature in the Student is superior to the Sufficiency of the Instructor; and it is not to be wonder'd at, for, if from time to time, even great Masters were not out-done, most of the finest Arts would have sunk before now.

§ 50. It may seem to many, that every perfect Singer must also be a perfect Instructor, but it is not so; for his Qualifications (though ever so great) are insufficient, if he cannot communicate his Sentiments with Ease, and in a Method adapted to the Ability of the Scholar; if he has not some Notion of Composition, and a manner of instructing, which may seem rather an Entertainment than a Lesson; with the happy Talent to shew the Ability of the Singer to Advantage, and conceal his Imperfections; which are the principal and most necessary Instructions.

§ 51. A Master, that is possessed of the above-mentioned Qualifications, is capable of Teaching; with them he will raise a Desire to study; will correct Errors with Reason; and by Examples incite a Taste to imitate him.

§ 52. He knows, that a Deficiency of Ornaments displeases as much as the too great Abundance of them; that a Singer makes one languid and dull with too little, and cloys one with too much; but, of the two, he will dislike the former most, though it gives less Offence, the latter being easier to be amended.

§ 53. He will have no Manner of Esteem for those who have no other Graces than gradual *Divisions* *; and will tell you, Embellishments of this Sort are only fit for Beginners.

§ 54. He will have as little Esteem for those who think to make their Auditors faint away, with their Transition from the sharp Third to the Flat.

§ 55. He'll tell you, that a Singer is lazy, who on the Stage, from Night to Night, teaches the Audience all his Songs; who, by hearing them always without the least Variation, have no Difficulty to learn them by Heart.

§ 56. He will be affrighted at the Rashness of one that launches out, with little Practice, and less Study; lest venturing too far, he should be in great Danger of losing himself.

§ 53. * *Passo* and *Passagio*. The Difference is, that a *Passo* is a sudden Grace or Flight, not uniform. See Pl. VI. Numb. 5. A *Passagio* is a Division, a Continuation, or a Succession of Notes, ascending or descending with Uniformity. See Pl. VI. Numb. 6.

§ 57. He will not praise one that presumes to sing two Parts in three of an Opera, promising himself never to be tiresome, as if that divine Privilege of always pleasing were allowed him here below. Such a one does not know the first Principle of musical Politicks; but Time will teach it him. He, that sings little and well, sings very well.

§ 58. He will laugh at those who imagine to satisfy the Publick with the Magnificence of their Habits, without reflecting, that Merit and Ignorance are equally aggrandized by Pomp. The Singers, that have nothing but the outward Appearance, pay that Debt to the Eyes, which they owe to the Ears.

§ 59. He will nauseate the new-invented Stile of those who provoke the innocent Notes with coarse Startings of the Voice. A disagreable Defect; however, being brought from

§ 59. This alludes to the *French* Manner of Singing, from whence that Defect is copy'd.

beyond the *Alps*, it passes for a *modern* Rarity.

§ 60. He will be astonished at this bewitched Age, in which so many are paid so well for singing ill. The *Moderns* would not be pleas'd to be put in Mind, that, twenty Years ago, indifferent Singers had but mean Parts allotted them, even in the secondrate Theatres; whereas at present, those, who are taught like Parrots, heap up Treasures beyond what the Singers of the first Degree then did.

§ 61. He will condemn the Ignorance of the Men most, they being more obliged to study than the Women.

§ 62. He will not bear with one who imitates the Women, even in sacrificing the Time, in order to acquire the Title of *Modern*.

§ 63. He will marvel at that Singer, who, having a good Knowledge of Time, yet does not make use of it, for want of having apply'd himself to the Study of Composition, or to accompany himself. His Mistake makes him think, that, to be eminent, it suffices to sing at Sight; and does not perceive that the greatest Difficulty, and the whole Beauty of the Profession consists in what he is ignorant of; he wants that Art which teaches to anticipate the Time, knowing where to lose it again; and, which is still more charming, to know how to lose it, in order to recover it again; which are the Advantages of such as understand Composition, and have the best Taste.

§ 64. He will be displeased at the Presumption of a Singer who gets the Words of the most wanton *Airs* of the Theatre rendered into *Latin*, that he may sing them with Applause in the

§ 60. The Time he alludes to, is at present between thirty and forty Years ago.

§ 63. Compare this Section with Section 41 in this Chapter and the Note.

§ 64. This is a Fault more than once heard of, in *Oratorio's* or *Motetts*.

Church; as if there were no Manner of Difference between the Stile of the one and the other; and, as if the Scraps of the Stage were fit to offer to the Deity.

§ 65. What will he not say of him who has found out the prodigious Art of Singing like a *Cricket?* Who could have ever imagin'd, before the Introduction of the *Mode*, that ten or a dozen Quavers in a Row could be trundled along one after another, with a Sort of *Tremor* of the Voice, which for some time past has gone under the Name of *Mordente Fresco?*

§ 66. He will have a still greater Detestation for the Invention of Laughing in Singing, or that screaming like a Hen when she is laying her Egg. Will there not be some other little Animal worth their Imitation, in order to make the Profession more and more ridiculous?

§ 67. He will disapprove the malicious Custom of a Singer in Repute, who talks and laughs on the Stage with his Companions, to induce the Publick to believe that such a Singer, who appears the first time on the Stage, does not deserve his Attention; when in reality he is afraid of, or envies, his gaining Applause.

§ 68. He cannot endure the Vanity of that Singer, who, full of himself from the little he has learned, is so taken with his own Performance, that he seems falling into an Extasy; pretending to impose Silence and create Wonder, as if his first Note said to the Audience, *Hear and Die:* But they, unwilling to die, chuse not to hear him, talk loud, and perhaps not much to his Advantage. At his second Air the Noise encreases, and still encreasing, he looks upon it as a manifest Injury done him; and, instead of correcting his conceited Pride by Study, he curses the deprav'd Taste of that Nation that does not esteem him, menacing never to return again; and thus the vain Wretch comforts himself.

§ 65. See Example, Pl. VI. Numb. 7.

§ 69. He will laugh at one who will not act unless he has the Choice of the Drama, and a Composer to his liking; with this additional Condition, not to sing in Company with such a Man, or without such a Woman.

§ 70. With the like Derision, he will observe some others, who with an Humility worse than Pride, go from one Box to another, gathering Praises from the most illustrious Persons, under a Pretence of a most profound Obsequiousness, and become in every Representation more and more familiar. Humility and Modesty are most beautiful Virtues; but if they are not accompanied with a little Decorum, they have some Resemblance to Hypocrisy.

§ 71. He will have no great Opinion of one, who is not satisfied with his Part, and never learns it; of one, who never sings in an Opera without thrusting in one *Air* which he always carries in his Pocket; of one, who bribes the Composer to give him an *Air* that was intended for another; of one, who takes Pains about Trifles, and neglects Things of Importance; of one, who, by procuring undeserved Recommendations, makes himself and his Patron ridiculous; of one, who does not sustain his Voice, out of Aversion to the *Pathetick*; of one, who gallops to follow the *Mode*; and of all the bad Singers, who, not knowing what's good, court the *Mode* to learn its Defects.

§ 72. To sum up all, he will call none a Singer of Merit, but him who is correct; and who executes with a Variety of Graces of his own, which his Skill inspires him with unpremeditately; knowing, that a Professor of Eminence cannot, if he would, continually repeat an *Air* with the self-same *Passages* and *Graces*. He who sings premeditately, shews he has learn'd his Lesson at Home.

§ 73. After having corrected several other Abuses and Defects, to the Advantage of the Singer, he will return with stronger Reasons to persuade him to have Recourse to the fundamental

mental Rules, which will teach him to proceed on the Bass from one Interval to another, with sure Steps, and without Danger of erring. If then the Singer should say, Sir, you trouble yourself in vain, for the bare Knowledge of the Errors is not sufficient; I have need of other Help than Words, and I know not where to find it, since it seems that there is at present such a Scarcity of good Examples in *Italy*: Then, shrugging his Shoulders, he will answer him, rather with Sighs than Words; that he must endeavour to learn of the best Singers that there are; particularly by observing two of the fair Sex, * of a Me-

§ 73. * *Faustina* and *Cuzzoni*, they both having within these few Years been in *England*, there needs no other Remark to be made on them, but to inform Futurity, that the *English* Audience distinguish'd them Both and at the same time, according to their Merit, and as our Author has describ'd them.

It may be worth remarking, that *Castilione*, who lived above two hundred Years ago, in his *Cortegiano*, describes *Bidon*, and *Marchetto Cara*, two

a Merit superior to all Praise; who with equal Force, in a different Stile, help to keep up the tottering Profession from immediately falling into Ruin. The one is inimitable for a privileg'd Gift of Singing, and for enchanting the World with a prodigious Felicity in executing, and with a singular Brillant, (I know not whether from Nature or Art) which pleases to Excess. The delightful soothing *Cantabile* of the other, joined with the Sweetness of a fine Voice, a perfect Intonation, Strictness of Time, and the rarest Productions of a Genius, are Qualifications as particular and uncommon, as they are difficult to be imitated. The *Pathetick* of the one, and the *Allegro* of the other, are the Qualities the most to be admired respectively in each of them. What a beautiful Mixture would it be, if the Excellence of these two angelick Creatures could be united in one single

two famous Singers in his Time, with the same distinguishing Qualifications.

Person! But let us not lose Sight of the Master.

§ 74. He will also convince the Scholar, that the Artifice of a Professor is never more pleasing, than when he deceives the Audience with agreable Surprizes; for which reason he will advise him to have Recourse to a seeming Plainness, as if he aim'd at nothing else.

§ 75. But when the Audience is in no farther Expectation, and (as I may say) grows indolent, he will direct him to rouse them that Instant with a *Grace*.

§ 76. When they are again awake, he will direct him to return to his feigned Simplicity, though it will no more be in his Power to delude those that hear him, for with an impatient Curiosity they already expect a second, and so on.

§ 77. He will give him ample Instructions concerning *Graces* of all sorts, and furnish him with Rules and profitable Documents.

§ 78. Here should I inveigh (though I could not enough) against the Treachery of my Memory, that has not preserved, as it ought, all those peculiar Excellencies which a great Man did once communicate to me, concerning *Passages* and *Graces*; and to my great Sorrow, and perhaps to the Loss of others, it will not serve me to publish any more than these few poor Remains, the Impressions of which are still left, and which I am now going to mention.

CHAP. X.

Of Passages *or* Graces.

Assages or *Graces* being the principal Ornaments in Singing, and the most favourite Delight of the Judicious, it is proper that the Singer be very attentive to learn this Art.

§ 2. Therefore let him know, that there are five principal Qualifications, which being united, will bring him to admirable Perfection, *viz. Judgment, Invention, Time, Art,* and *Taste.*

§ 3. There are likewise five subaltern Embellishments *viz.* the *Appoggiatura,* the *Shake,* the *putting forth of the Voice,* the *Gliding,* and *Dragging.*

The principal Qualifications teach,

§ 4. That the *Passages* and *Graces* cannot be form'd but from a profound *Judgment.*

§ 5. That they are produced by a singular and beautiful *Invention,* remote from all that is vulgar and common.

§ 6. That, being govern'd by the rigorous, but necessary, Precepts of *Time,* they never transgress its regulated Measure, without losing their own Merit.

§ 7. That, being guided by the most refined *Art* on the Bass, they may There (and no where else) find their Center; there to sport with Delight, and unexpectedly to charm.

§ 8. That, it is owing to an exquisite *Taste,* that they are executed with that sweet *putting forth* of the Voice, which is so enchanting.

From the accessary Qualities is learn'd,

§ 9. That the *Graces* or *Passages* be easy in Appearance, thereby to give universal Delight.

§ 10. That in effect They be difficult, that thereby the Art of the Inventor be the more admired.

§ 11. That They be performed with an equal regard to the Expression of the Words, and the Beauty of the Art.

§ 12. That They be *gliding* or *dragging* in the *Pathetick*, for They have a better Effect than those that are mark'd.

§ 13. That They do not appear studied, in order to be the more regarded.

§ 14. That They be softened with the *Piano* in the *Pathetick*, which will make them more affecting.

§ 15. That in the *Allegro* They be sometimes accompanied with the *Forte* and the *Piano*, so as to make a sort of *Chiaro Scuro*.

§ 16. That They be confin'd to a *Group* of few Notes, which are more pleasing than those which are too numerous.

§ 17. That in a slow *Time*, there may be a greater Number of them (if the Bass allows it) with an Obligation upon the Singer to keep to the Point propos'd, that his Capacity be made more conspicuous.

§ 18. That They be properly introduc'd, for in a wrong Place They disgust.

§ 19. That They come not too close together, in order to keep them distinct.

§ 20. That They should proceed rather from the Heart than from the Voice, in order to make their way to the Heart more easily.

§ 21. That They be not made on the second or fourth Vowel, when closely pronounc'd, and much less on the third and fifth.

§ 22. That They be not copied, if you would not have them appear defective.

§ 23. That They be stol'n on the *Time*, to captivate the Soul.

§ 24. That They never be repeated in the same place, particularly in *Pathetick Airs*, for there they are the most

moſt taken Notice of by the Judicious.

§ 25. And, above all, let them be improv'd; by no means let them loſe in the Repetition.

§ 26. Many Profeſſors are of Opinion, that in *Graces* there is no room for the mark'd *Diviſions*, unleſs mix'd with ſome of the aforeſaid Embelliſhments, or ſome other agreable Accidents.

§ 27. But it is now time that we ſpeak of the *Dragging*, that, if the *Pathetick* ſhould once return again into the World, a Singer might be able to underſtand it. The Explanation would be eaſier underſtood by Notes of Muſick than by Words, if the Printer was not under great Difficulty to print a few Notes; notwithſtanding which, I'll endeavour, the beſt I can, to make myſelf underſtood.

§ 28. When on an even and regular Movement of a Baſs, which proceeds ſlowly, a Singer begins with a high Note, dragging it gently down to a low one, with the *Forte* and *Piano*, almoſt gradually, with Inequality of Motion, that is to ſay, ſtopping a little more on ſome Notes in the Middle, than on thoſe that begin or end the *Straſcino* or *Dragg**. Every good Muſician takes it for granted, that in the Art of Singing there is no Invention ſuperior, or Execution more apt to touch the Heart than this, provided however it be done with Judgment, and with putting forth of the Voice in a juſt *Time* on the Baſs. Whoſoever has moſt Notes at Command, has the greater Advantage; becauſe this pleaſing Ornament is ſo much the more to be admired, by how much the greater the Fall is. Perform'd by an excellent *Soprano*, that makes uſe of it but ſeldom, it becomes a Prodigy; but as much as it pleaſes deſcending, no leſs would it diſpleaſe aſcending.

§ 29. Mind this, O my beloved Singers! For it is to You only, who are inclined to ſtudy, that I have addreſſed myſelf. This was the Doctrine of the School of thoſe Profeſſors,

---

§ 28. * See Examples, Pl. VI. Numb. 8 and 9.

sors, whom, by way of Reproach, some mistaken Persons call *Ancients*. Observe carefully its Rules, examine strictly its Precepts, and, if not blinded by Prejudice, you will see that this School ought to sing in Tune, to put forth the Voice, to make the Words understood, to express, to use proper Gesture, to perform in *Time*, to vary on its Movement, to compose, and to study the *Pathetick*, in which alone Taste and Judgment triumph. Confront this School with yours, and if its Precepts should not be sufficient to instruct you, learn what's wanting from the *Modern*.

§ 30. But if these my Exhortations, proceeding from my Zeal, have no Weight with you, as the Advice of Inferiors is seldom regarded, allow at least, that whoever has the Faculty of Thinking, may once in sixty Years think right. And if you think, that I have been too partial to the Times past, then would I persuade you, (if you have not a shaking Hand) to weigh in a just Ballance your most renowned Singers; who you take to be *Moderns*, but are not so, except in their *Cadences*;) and having undeceived yourselves, you will perceive in them, that instead of Affectations, Abuses, and Errors, They sing according to those powerful Lessons that give Delight to the Soul, and whose Perfections have made Impressions on me, and which I shall always remember with the greatest Pleasure. Do but consult them, as I have done, and they will truly and freely tell you, That They sell their Jewels where they are understood; That the Singers of Eminence are not of the *Mode*, and that at present there are many bad Singers.

§ 31. True it is, that there are some, tho' few, very good Singers, who, when the Vehemence of their youthful Fire is abated, will by their Examples do Justice to their delightful Profession, in keeping up the Splendor of it, and will leave to Posterity a lasting and glorious Fame of their Performances. I point them out to you, that, if you find yourselves in an Error,

Error, you may not want the Means to correct it, nor an Oracle to apply to whenever you have occasion. From whence I have good Grounds to hope, that the true Taste in Singing will last to the End of the World.

§ 32. Whoever comprehends what has been demonstrated to him, in these and many other Observations, will need no farther Incitement to study. Stirred up by his own Desire, he will fly to his beloved Instrument, from which, by continued Application, he will find he has no Reason to sit down satisfied with what he has learn'd before. He will make new Discoveries, inventing new Graces, from whence after comparing them well together, he will chuse the best, and will make use of them as long as he thinks them so; but, going on in refining, he will find others more deserving his Esteem. To conclude, from these he will proceed on to an almost infinite Number of *Graces*, by the means whereof his Mind will be so opened, that the most hidden Treasures of the Art, and most remote from his Imagination, will voluntarily present themselves; so that, unless Pride blinds him, or Study becomes tiresome to him, or his Memory fails him, he will encrease his Store of Embellishments, in a Stile which will be entirely his own: The principal Aim of one that strives to gain the highest Applause.

§ 33. Finally, O ye young Singers, hearken to me for your Profit and Advantage. The Abuses, the Defects, and the Errors divulg'd by me in these Observations, (which in Justice ought not to be charg'd on the *Modern* Stile) were once almost all Faults I myself was guilty of; and in the Flower of my Youth, when I thought myself to be a Great Man, it was not easy for me to discover them. But, in a more mature Age, the slow Undeceit comes too late. I know I have sung ill, and 'would I have not writ worse! but since I have suffered by my Ignorance, let it at least serve for a Warning to amend those who wish to sing well. He that studies, let him imitate the ingenious Bee, that sucks its Honey from the moſt grateful Flowers. From thoſe called *Ancients*, and thoſe ſuppoſed *Moderns*, (as I have ſaid) much may be learn'd; it is enough to find out the Flower, and know how to diſtill, and draw the Eſſence from it.

§ 34. The moſt cordial, and not leſs profitable Advice, I can give you, is the following:

§ 35. Remember what has been wiſely obſerved, that Mediocrity of Merit can but for a ſhort time eclipſe the true Sublime, which, how old ſoever it grows, can never die.

§ 36. Abhor the Example of thoſe who hate Correction; for like Lightning to thoſe who walk in the Dark, tho' it frightens them, it gives them Light.

§ 37. Learn from the Errors of others: O great Leſſon! it coſts little, and inſtructs much. Of every one ſomething is to be learned, and the moſt Ignorant is ſometimes the greateſt Maſter.

F I N I S.

Music and Books published by Travis & Emery Music Bookshop:
Anon.: Hymnarium Sarisburiense, cum Rubricis et Notis Musicis.
Agricola, Johann Friedrich from Tosi: Anleitung zur Singkunst.
Bach, C.P.E.: edited W. Emery: Nekrolog or Obituary Notice of J.S. Bach.
Bateson, Naomi Judith: Alcock of Salisbury
Bathe, William: A Briefe Introduction to the Skill of Song
Bax, Arnold: Symphony #5, Arranged for Piano Four Hands by Walter Emery
Burney, Charles: The Present State of Music in France and Italy
Burney, Charles: The Present State of Music in Germany, The Netherlands …
Burney, Charles: An Account of the Musical Performances ... Handel
Burney, Karl: Nachricht von Georg Friedrich Handel's Lebensumstanden.
Burns, Robert: The Caledonian Musical Museum ..The Best Scotch Songs. (1810)
Cobbett, W.W.: Cobbett's Cyclopedic Survey of Chamber Music. (2 vols.)
Corrette, Michel: Le Maitre de Clavecin
Crimp, Bryan: Dear Mr. Rosenthal … Dear Mr. Gaisberg …
Crimp, Bryan: Solo: The Biography of Solomon
d'Indy, Vincent: Beethoven: Biographie Critique
d'Indy, Vincent: Beethoven: A Critical Biography
d'Indy, Vincent: César Franck (in French)
Fischhof, Joseph: Versuch einer Geschichte des Clavierbaues. (Faksimile 1853).
Frescobaldi, Girolamo: D'Arie Musicali per Cantarsi. Primo & Secondo Libro.
Geminiani, Francesco: The Art of Playing the Violin.
Handel; Purcell; Boyce; Geene et al: Calliope or English Harmony: Volume First.
Häuser: Musikalisches Lexikon. 2 vols in one.
Hawkins, John: A General History of the Science and Practice of Music (5 vols.)
Herbert-Caesari, Edgar: The Science and Sensations of Vocal Tone
Herbert-Caesari, Edgar: Vocal Truth
Hopkins and Rimboult: The Organ. Its History and Construction.
Hunt, John: - see separate list of discographies at the end of these titles
Isaacs, Lewis: Hänsel and Gretel. A Guide to Humperdinck's Opera.
Isaacs, Lewis: Königskinder (Royal Children) A Guide to Humperdinck's Opera.
Kastner: Manuel Général de Musique Militaire
Lacassagne, M. l'Abbé Joseph : Traité Général des élémens du Chant.
Lascelles (née Catley), Anne: The Life of Miss Anne Catley.
Mainwaring, John: Memoirs of the Life of the Late George Frederic Handel
Malcolm, Alexander: A Treaty of Music: Speculative, Practical and Historical
Marx, Adolph Bernhard: Die Kunst des Gesanges, Theoretisch-Practisch
May, Florence: The Life of Brahms
May, Florence: The Girlhood Of Clara Schumann: Clara Wieck And Her Time.
Mellers, Wilfrid: Angels of the Night: Popular Female Singers of Our Time
Mellers, Wilfrid: Bach and the Dance of God
Mellers, Wilfrid: Beethoven and the Voice of God
Mellers, Wilfrid: Caliban Reborn - Renewal in Twentieth Century Music

Music and Books published by Travis & Emery Music Bookshop:

Mellers, Wilfrid: Darker Shade of Pale, A Backdrop to Bob Dylan
Mellers, Wilfrid: François Couperin and the French Classical Tradition
Mellers, Wilfrid: Harmonious Meeting
Mellers, Wilfrid: Le Jardin Retrouvé, The Music of Frederic Mompou
Mellers, Wilfrid: Music and Society, England and the European Tradition
Mellers, Wilfrid: Music in a New Found Land: … … American Music
Mellers, Wilfrid: Romanticism and the Twentieth Century (from 1800)
Mellers, Wilfrid: The Masks of Orpheus: …… the Story of European Music.
Mellers, Wilfrid: The Sonata Principle (from c. 1750)
Mellers, Wilfrid: Vaughan Williams and the Vision of Albion
Panchianio, Cattuffio: Rutzvanscad Il Giovine
Pearce, Charles: Sims Reeves, Fifty Years of Music in England.
Playford, John: An Introduction to the Skill of Musick.
Purcell, Henry et al: Harmonia Sacra … The First Book, (1726)
Purcell, Henry et al: Harmonia Sacra … Book II (1726)
Quantz, Johann: Versuch einer Anweisung die Flöte trave rsiere zu spielen.
Rameau, Jean-Philippe: Code de Musique Pratique, ou Methodes.
Rastall, Richard: The Notation of Western Music.
Rimbault, Edward: The Pianoforte, Its Origins, Progress, and Construction.
Rousseau, Jean Jacques: Dictionnaire de Musique
Rubinstein, Anton : Guide to the proper use of the Pianoforte Pedals.
Sainsbury, John S.: Dictionary of Musicians. (1825). 2 vols.
Serré de Rieux, Jean de : Les dons des Enfans de Latone
Simpson, Christopher: A Compendium of Practical Musick in Five Parts
Spohr, Louis: Autobiography
Spohr, Louis: Grand Violin School
Tans'ur, William: A New Musical Grammar; or The Harmonical Spectator
Terry, Charles Sanford: Bach's Chorals – Parts 1, 2 and 3.
Terry, Charles Sanford: John Christian Bach
Terry, Charles Sanford: J.S. Bach's Original Hymn-Tunes for Congregational Use.
Terry, Charles Sanford: Four-Part Chorals of J.S. Bach. (German & English)
Terry, Charles Sanford: Joh. Seb. Bach, Cantata Texts, Sacred and Secular.
Terry, Charles Sanford: The Origins of the Family of Bach Musicians.
Tosi, Pierfrancesco: Opinioni de' Cantori Antichi, e Moderni
Tosi, Pierfrancesco: Observations on the Florid Song.
Van der Straeten, Edmund: History of the Violoncello, The Viol da Gamba …
Van der Straeten, Edmund: History of the Violin, Its Ancestors… (2 vols.)
Walther, J. G. [Waltern]: Musicalisches Lexikon [Musikalisches Lexicon]
Zwirn, Gerald: Stranded Stories From The Operas

Travis & Emery Music Bookshop
17 Cecil Court, London, WC2N 4EZ, United Kingdom.
Tel. (+44) 20 7240 2129

© Travis & Emery 2010

Discographies by Travis & Emery:
Discographies by John Hunt.

1987: 978-1-906857-14-1: From Adam to Webern: the Recordings of von Karajan.
1991: 978-0-951026-83-0: 3 Italian Conductors and 7 Viennese Sopranos: 10 Discographies: Arturo Toscanini, Guido Cantelli, Carlo Maria Giulini, Elisabeth Schwarzkopf, Irmgard Seefried, Elisabeth Gruemmer, Sena Jurinac, Hilde Gueden, Lisa Della Casa, Rita Streich.
1992: 978-0-951026-85-4: Mid-Century Conductors and More Viennese Singers: 10 Discographies: Karl Boehm, Victor De Sabata, Hans Knappertsbusch, Tullio Serafin, Clemens Krauss, Anton Dermota, Leonie Rysanek, Eberhard Waechter, Maria Reining, Erich Kunz.
1993: 978-0-951026-87-8: More 20th Century Conductors: 7 Discographies: Eugen Jochum, Ferenc Fricsay, Carl Schuricht, Felix Weingartner, Josef Krips, Otto Klemperer, Erich Kleiber.
1994: 978-0-951026-88-5: Giants of the Keyboard: 6 Discographies: Wilhelm Kempff, Walter Gieseking, Edwin Fischer, Clara Haskil, Wilhelm Backhaus, Artur Schnabel.
1994: 978-0-951026-89-2: Six Wagnerian Sopranos: 6 Discographies: Frieda Leider, Kirsten Flagstad, Astrid Varnay, Martha Moedl, Birgit Nilsson, Gwyneth Jones.
1995: 978-0-952582-70-0: Musical Knights: 6 Discographies: Henry Wood, Thomas Beecham, Adrian Boult, John Barbirolli, Reginald Goodall, Malcolm Sargent.
1995: 978-0-952582-71-7: A Notable Quartet: 4 Discographies: Gundula Janowitz, Christa Ludwig, Nicolai Gedda, Dietrich Fischer-Dieskau.
1996: 978-0-952582-75-5: Leopold Stokowski (1882-1977): Discography and Concert Register
1996: 978-0-952582-76-2: Makers of the Philharmonia: 11 Discographies: Alceo Galliera, Walter Susskind, Paul Kletzki, Nicolai Malko, Issay Dobrowen, Lovro Von Matacic, Efrem Kurtz, Otto Ackermann, Anatole Fistoulari, George Weldon, Robert Irving.
1996: 978-0-952582-72-4: The Post-War German Tradition: 5 Discographies: Rudolf Kempe, Joseph Keilberth, Wolfgang Sawallisch, Rafael Kubelik, Andre Cluytens.
1996: 978-0-952582-73-1: Teachers and Pupils: 7 Discographies: Elisabeth Schwarzkopf, Maria Ivoguen, Maria Cebotari, Meta Seinemeyer, Ljuba Welitsch, Rita Streich, Erna Berger.
1996: 978-0-952582-75-5: Leopold Stokowski: Discography and Concert Listing.
1996: 978-0-952582-76-2: Makers of the Philharmonia: 11 Discographies Alceo Galliera, Walter Susskind, Paul Kletzki, Nicolai Malko, Issay Dobrowen, Lovro Von Matacic, Efrem Kurtz, Otto Ackermann, Anatole Fistoulari, George Weldon, Robert Irving.
1996: 978-0-952582-77-9: Tenors in a Lyric Tradition: 3 Discographies: Peter Anders, Walther Ludwig, Fritz Wunderlich.
1997: 978-0-952582-78-6: The Lyric Baritone: 5 Discographies: Hans Reinmar, Gerhard Huesch, Josef Metternich, Hermann Uhde, Eberhard Waechter.
1997: 978-0-952582-79-3: Hungarians in Exile: 3 Discographies: Fritz Reiner, Antal Dorati, George Szell.
1997: 978-1-901395-00-6: The Art of the Diva: 3 Discographies: Claudia Muzio, Maria Callas, Magda Olivero.
1997: 978-1-901395-01-3: Metropolitan Sopranos: 4 Discographies: Rosa Ponselle, Eleanor Steber, Zinka Milanov, Leontyne Price.
1997: 978-1-901395-02-0: Back From The Shadows: 4 Discographies: Willem Mengelberg, Dimitri Mitropoulos, Hermann Abendroth, Eduard Van Beinum.
1997: 978-1-901395-03-7: More Musical Knights: 4 Discographies: Hamilton Harty, Charles Mackerras, Simon Rattle, John Pritchard.
1998: 978-1-901395-95-2: More Giants of the Keyboard: 5 Discographies: Claudio Arrau, Gyorgy Cziffra, Vladimir Horowitz, Dinu Lipatti, Artur Rubinstein.

1998: 978-1-901395-94-5: Conductors On The Yellow Label: 8 Discographies: Fritz Lehmann, Ferdinand Leitner, Ferenc Fricsay, Eugen Jochum, Leopold Ludwig, Artur Rother, Franz Konwitschny, Igor Markevitch.

1998: 978-1-901395-96-9: Mezzo and Contraltos: 5 Discographies: Janet Baker, Margarete Klose, Kathleen Ferrier, Giulietta Simionato, Elisabeth Hoengen.

1999: 978-1-901395-97-6: The Furtwaengler Sound Sixth Edition: Discography and Concert Listing.

1999: 978-1-901395-98-3: The Great Dictators: 3 Discographies: Evgeny Mravinsky, Artur Rodzinski, Sergiu Celibidache.

1999: 978-1-901395-99-0: Sviatoslav Richter: Pianist of the Century: Discography.

2000: 978-1-901395-04-4: Philharmonic Autocrat 1: Discography of: Herbert Von Karajan [Third Edition].

2000: 978-1-901395-05-1: Wiener Philharmoniker 1 - Vienna Philharmonic and Vienna State Opera Orchestras: Discography Part 1 1905-1954.

2000: 978-1-901395-06-8: Wiener Philharmoniker 2 - Vienna Philharmonic and Vienna State Opera Orchestras: Discography Part 2 1954-1989.

2001: 978-1-901395-07-5: Gramophone Stalwarts: 3 Separate Discographies: Bruno Walter, Erich Leinsdorf, Georg Solti.

2001: 978-1-901395-08-2: Singers of the Third Reich: 5 Discographies: Helge Roswaenge, Tiana Lemnitz, Franz Voelker, Maria Mueller, Max Lorenz.

2001: 978-1-901395-09-9: Philharmonic Autocrat 2: Concert Register of Herbert Von Karajan Second Edition.

2002: 978-1-901395-10-5: Sächsische Staatskapelle Dresden: Complete Discography.

2002: 978-1-901395-11-2: Carlo Maria Giulini: Discography and Concert Register.

2002: 978-1-901395-12-9: Pianists For The Connoisseur: 6 Discographies: Arturo Benedetti Michelangeli, Alfred Cortot, Alexis Weissenberg, Clifford Curzon, Solomon, Elly Ney.

2003: 978-1-901395-14-3: Singers on the Yellow Label: 7 Discographies: Maria Stader, Elfriede Troetschel, Annelies Kupper, Wolfgang Windgassen, Ernst Haefliger, Josef Greindl, Kim Borg.

2003: 978-1-901395-15-0: A Gallic Trio: 3 Discographies: Charles Muench, Paul Paray, Pierre Monteux.

2004: 978-1-901395-16-7: Antal Dorati 1906-1988: Discography and Concert Register.

2004: 978-1-901395-17-4: Columbia 33CX Label Discography.

2004: 978-1-901395-18-1: Great Violinists: 3 Discographies: David Oistrakh, Wolfgang Schneiderhan, Arthur Grumiaux.

2006: 978-1-901395-19-8: Leopold Stokowski: Second Edition of the Discography.

2006: 978-1-901395-20-4: Wagner Im Festspielhaus: Discography of the Bayreuth Festival.

2006: 978-1-901395-21-1: Her Master's Voice: Concert Register and Discography of Dame Elisabeth Schwarzkopf [Third Edition].

2007: 978-1-901395-22-8: Hans Knappertsbusch: Kna: Concert Register and Discography of Hans Knappertsbusch, 1888-1965. Second Edition.

2008: 978-1-901395-23-5: Philips Minigroove: Second Extended Version of the European Discography.

2009: 978-1-901395-24-2: American Classics: The Discographies of Leonard Bernstein and Eugene Ormandy.

2010: 978-1-901395-25-9: Dirigenten der DDR: Conductors of the German Democratic Republic

Discography by Stephen J. Pettitt, edited by John Hunt:

1987: 978-1-906857-16-5: Philharmonia Orchestra: Complete Discography 1945-1987

Available from: Travis & Emery at 17 Cecil Court, London, UK. (+44) 20 7 240 2129. email on sales@travis-and-emery.com .

© Travis & Emery 2010